Tanzania: The Land and Its People

John Ndembwike

1

Tanzania: The Land and Its People
John Ndembwike

Second Edition

ISBN-10: 0-9802534-4-6
ISBN-13: 978-0-9802534-4-3

New Africa Press
Dar es Salaam, Tanzania
Pretoria, South Africa

Contents

About the Author

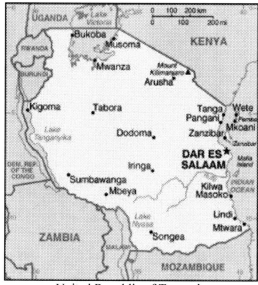

United Republic of Tanzania

Tanzania in a larger East African context.

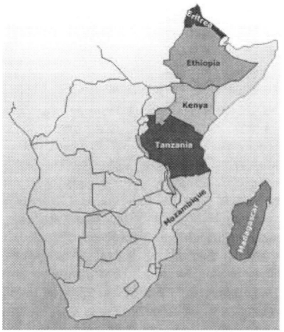

Tanzania in Eastern and Southern Africa.

Introduction

THIS book is intended to introduce Tanzania to people around the world who don't know much about this East African country.

It can also be used as an introductory text in high school and in college. It is intended for members of the general public as much as it is for the academic community. Included are appendices on the East African Community (EAC) and prospects for an East African federation.

Many people know about Mount Kilimanjaro, the highest mountain in Africa. But there are many things about Tanzania which many people don't know about. In fact, some don't even know that the snow-capped Mount Kilimanjaro is in Tanzania. They think or have been misled, sometimes deliberately, to believe that it is in Kenya, a neighbouring country.

Also, probably most people, including Tanzanians themselves as well as other Africans, don't know that Tanzania has more inland waters than any other African country. It also has the greatest variation in altitude on the continent from sea level to the peaks of Kilimanjaro and other mountainous areas especially on the mainland.

And it is not just a land of large national parks and game reserves which attract hundreds of thousands of visitors to this "garden of Eden" from all over the world every year. It is true we have Serengeti, known worldwide and made even more famous by John Wayne in his film "Hatari," which means danger in Kiswahili, shot when the famous American actor and his crew came to Tanganyika in 1962.

But Tanzania has a lot more than that. It has a rich history, an impressive ethnic, racial and cultural diversity, and great economic potential among many other things. It is also known for its peace and stability and stunning beauty.

I hope that this book will help you to learn more about Tanzania which also includes an area that is considered to be the cradle of mankind.

Chapter One:

Historical Background

TANZANIA is the largest country in a region that is generally known as East Africa.

The other countries in the region are Kenya and Uganda and they all were once ruled by Britain.

Tanzania is also known as the origin of mankind following the discovery of human-like fossil remains by British anthropologists, Dr. L.S.B. Leakey and his wife Mary, in the Olduvai Gorge in Ngorongoro Crater in 1959 in what was then northern Tanganyika before the country was renamed Tanzania in 1964.

Dr. Leakey's interest was sparked by earlier findings of some fossils and bones by a German entomologist in 1910 in the Olduvai Gorge which showed evidence of human life in the area. Leakey and his wife Mary, both of whom were Kenyans, started doing research in the Olduvai Gorge in 1931.

But it was not until 1959 that they had their major finding when Mary Leakey found fragments of teeth and a skull which were identified as remains of a male hominid whom they named Zinjanthropus, or Nutcracker Man, because of his extraordinarily large teeth.

About 20 years later, they found footprints at Laetoli, an area south of Olduvai, further validating their findings as proof of the presence of hominids in the region which earned it distinction as the origin of mankind. As Paul Rincon stated on BBC News years later:

New DNA evidence suggests "African Eve", the 150,000-year-old female ancestor of every person on Earth, may have lived in Tanzania or Ethiopia. A genetic study has shown that the oldest known human DNA lineages are those of East Africans. The most ancient populations include the Sandawe, Burunge, Gorowa and Datoga people who live in Tanzania.

Competing claims have come from other parts of East Africa, especially from Kenya and Ethiopia as the origin of mankind, but they have not dethroned Tanzania from its "eminent" status as the first home of the human species.

They, instead, as East African countries share together the distinction of East Africa as a region which is generally considered by scientists and anthropologists to be the original home of mankind, roughly equivalent to the Biblical Garden of Eden whose original site has never been located but which is probably in what is Iraq today based on the Biblical account of the land of Mesopotamia, the ancient name of Iraq, and of the ancient rivers of Euphrates and Tigris which still flow today.

It all depends on what you believe in, evolution or intelligent design as the origin of life, about which nothing seems to have been resolved in the meeting of the minds from the two opposing camps which remain sharply divided on this highly contentious subject. And Tanzania has figured prominently in this debate since Dr. Leakey and his wife Mary discovered man's "earliest:" ancestor in the Olduvai Gorge in 1959.

But as a country, Tanzania did not exist or come into being until the late 1880s when Germany claimed the territory as its sphere of influence and named it *Deutsch*

Ostafrika, which means German East Africa, an area which included what is now Rwanda and Burundi and what was then known as Ruanda-Urundi.

The area of what is Tanzania today is believed to have been first inhabited by people related to the Khoikhoi of the Kalahari desert. They were later overpowered and overwhelmed by immigrants from West Africa, the ancestors of most of the inhabitants of East Africa today who belong to the Bantu linguistic group and who are simply called Bantu.

The term "Bantu" was coined in the 1850s by W.H.I. Bleek, a librarian of the British government of the Cape colony in South Africa. It has acquired legitimacy ever since, although it is also highly controversial in some circles, for example in South Africa where it was used as a derogatory term during the apartheid era.

Most of the people in Tanzania are Bantu. There is overwhelming evidence from numerous archaeological findings in what is Tanzania today showing that large-scale immigration into the region took place about 2,000 years ago around 100 - 200 AD. The immigrants were mostly agriculturalists who emigrated from what is now Nigeria and Cameroon, especially from the border region between those two countries.

When these tribes or ethnic groups arrived in East Africa, including what is Tanzania today, they virtually expelled the indigenous people who were forced to move south where they eventually settled in the Kalahari desert and other parts of southern Africa.

More than one thousand places have been found in central Tanzania showing that the area was well-inhabited during the Stone Age. The findings include rock paintings especially in what is now Kondoa district and surrounding areas including Irangi.

Some of the original inhabitants still live in the area. They are the Hadzapi and the Sandawi, some of the smallest tribes in Tanzania, and whose languages including the click sound, have a striking resemblance to Khoisan, the language of the Khoikhoi - derisively called Hottentots - which is also related to the language of the San, so-called Bushmen; a linguistic affinity which binds these groups together as one people of common ancestry some of whom originated from an area that became Tanzania.

There were other immigrants who settled centuries ago in what is now Tanzania. In fact, they came long before the immigrants from West Africa arrived in the region.

In the second and first centuries BC, immigrants from the highlands of southern Ethiopia arrived and settled in Tanzania. They were Cushites and they settled mainly in the central part of what is now Tanzania.

Their descendants still live in Tanzania and constitute distinct groups, with their distinctive physical features and languages. These ethnic groups are the Iraqw, the Mbugu, the Burungi, and the Gorowa. They are also some of the smallest tribes in Tanzania.

Through the centuries, other immigration movements took place. More people immigrated into the region from West Africa.

Like the earlier immigrants, they were also agriculturalists and fashioned iron into implements for various activities including farming, cooking, and storage among others. They also made weapons - spears and arrows - from iron and they were, like the earlier immigrants from West Africa, of Bantu stock; a term used to describe members of ethnic groups who speak related languages even if some of these groups are not genetically related or there are major genetic differences between them.

Evidence of these iron-working Bantu immigrants from West Africa has been found in different parts of Tanzania including one important settlement at Engaruka north of Lake Manyara which has significant archaeological remains including more than 5,000 acres of cultivated and irrigated land.

Also various tools including axes from the Iron Age were found at Katuruka west of Bukoba in Kagera Region in northwestern Tanzania and at Isimila near Iringa in the Southern Highlands; critical evidence showing that Africans had for centuries used iron in their lives, skills that were handed down through the generations. Ironsmiths are common throughout Africa and have been an integral part of traditional African societies for centuries.

Besides vast immigration movements from West Africa, there were other migratory waves into the region from 300 - 400 AD. These were pastoral Nilotic tribes from the north who constitute a significant part of the population of Tanzania today. They are mostly found in northern parts of this vast East African country.

Other parts of Tanzania have also produced evidence of well-established communities and highly developed skills which existed centuries ago. For example, in the area of Uvinza in western Tanzania, there is evidence showing that salt mining dates from the early Stone Age. Pottery was also found in the same area dating from the 600s AD.

Salt traders established contacts beyond Lake Tanganyika in what became the Congo and carried on extensive trade for centuries until the 1800s. The decline in this commercial activity coincided with an increase in the slave trade by the Arabs which disrupted centuries-old patterns of African traditional life, and with the penetration of the African interior by Europeans which eventually led to the partition and colonisation of Africa after the Berlin Conference of 1885.

External contacts have also been an integral part of Tanzanian history for centuries. Before Tanzania was colonized by the Germans and by the British, the people along the coast already had commercial ties with Arab countries, especially Oman, and parts of Asia including India and China as well as Indonesia. A wave of immigrants reached the Tanzanian coast from Indonesia via Madagascar centuries ago. Others came straight from Indonesia.

Arabs settled in significant numbers along the coast in the 700s AD and through the years engaged in the slave trade many of whose victims were shipped to Mesopotamia, now Iraq, Arabia and other parts of the Arab world. African slaves were also sold to merchants in Persia, as Iran was known until 1935, India and even China as well as other parts of Asia including Indonesia.

And traders from India and southwest Asia had settled in the coastal areas of Tanzania by 900 AD. Commercial activities with Africans involved exchange of cloth, beads, porcelain and metal products for ivory and other items.

Shirazi immigrants from Persia also established settlements along the coast of what is now Tanzania from the 1100s - 1400s AD until they were supplanted and destroyed by the Portuguese in the 1500s AD.

The Arabs again gained prominence and reigned supreme along the coast from their stronghold in Zanzibar, replacing the Portuguese until they were finally conquered by the Germans. Resistance to brutal German rule which included land expropriation, forced labour, high taxation and corporal punishment, led to massive repression by the German colonial rulers.

Some of the most sustained resistance to German oppression and exploitation took place in the southern half of the country where Chief Mkwawa routed German forces more than once in his territory in Iringa in the Southern Highlands before he was finally defeated.

It was also in this part of the country - what is southern Tanzania today - where a number of tribes united to fight the Germans in the famous war that came to be known as Maji Maji.

The Germans almost lost the colony in this war and were rescued when they got reinforcements from Germany. About 200,000 people died during this campaign, mostly from disease and starvation.

The Germans pursued a scorched-earth policy, confiscating food, inflicting brutal punishment on the indigenous people including the destruction of villages. The result was massive famine and depopulation of vast expanses of territory and forced emigration of large numbers of people to other parts, many of which were inhospitable, hence unfit for human habitation.

The Maji Maji war of resistance was the bloodiest in the country's colonial history and one of the deadliest in the entire history of colonial Africa. The war was fought from 1905 to 1907. And between March and September 1906, all the leaders who spearheaded the Maji Maji war were hanged by the German authorities.

The Germans themselves lost the territory to the Allied forces in World War I, paving the way for the establishment of British rule with the blessings of the League of Nations in 1920. The country, formerly known as *Deutsch Ostafrika* or German East Africa, was renamed Tanganyika when the British took over. It was named after Lake Tanganyika.

It was such a tragedy that the country suffered so much in so short a time.

Not long after half of the country had virtually been destroyed during the Maji Maji war of resistance, came World War I only seven years later.

Vast areas of the country were devastated, turned into wasteland; economic life was disrupted; the social fabric of different tribes or ethnic groups was torn apart; rampant disease and extreme poverty further destroyed life; and thousands of African soldiers who had fought in the war succumbed to famine, malaria and other diseases.

The establishment of British colonial rule soon after the war ended did not alleviate the plight.

Compounding the problem was the fact that the British had no interest in investing in Tanganyika or in attracting large numbers of British settlers because it was not a colony like neighbouring Kenya which was a "White Man's Country," as Lord Delamere put it. By remarkable contrast, Tanganyika was supposed to be under British tutelage only for a period of time, although not specified, before it became independent.

But it was not until more than 40 years later that Tanganyika attained sovereign status after the British took over as the rulers of this vast East African country under the supervision of the League of Nations. In 1946, it became a UN trusteeship territory - simply known as Tanganyika Trust Territory - under British mandate, with the stipulation that Britain would eventually guide the country to independence.

Although the British had a "special responsibility" to Tanganyika to prepare the country for independence, they did not proceed at a pace that satisfied African nationalists. As Julius Nyerere said years later in the 1950s when he became the leader of the nationalist movement - Tanganyika African National Union (TANU) - fighting for independence, the colonial government and TANU were headed in the same direction but not at the same pace.

The colonial rulers did, however, encourage limited local government under the policy of indirect rule using traditional rulers to help administer vast expanses of territory, a policy first introduced by Sir Frederick Lugard, later Lord Lugard, in Northern Nigeria when he served there as British high commissioner from 1901 to 1906.

Under this system, the British colonial rulers delegated authority to the emirs and other traditional rulers in Northern Nigeria making them responsible for labour recruitment, tax collection and limited law enforcement in areas under their jurisdiction.

But the policy of indirect rule also led to conflict with African traditional values and ways of life and favoured the chiefs and other Africans who were loyal to the British rulers. It was, however, adopted throughout British colonial Africa and other parts of the continent under colonial rule as a way to minimize administrative cost and other expenses. Tanganyika was no exception.

In Tanganyika, as well as in some other parts of Africa, some of the African chiefs or traditional rulers were appointed by the colonial authorities, further alienating the people.

In 1922 the British authorities in Tanganyika authorized the formation of African organizations in pursuit of their "liberal" policy of allowing Africans to express their views and promote their well-being. But in reality, Africans did not enjoy much freedom since they were still colonial subjects and therefore not entitled to the same rights and privileges enjoyed by their rulers and other whites.

The most prominent of these organizations was the Tanganyika Territory African Civil Service Association which became the incubator of nationalist aspirations which culminated in the establishment of the Tanganyika African National Union (TANU) on 7 July 1954 under the leadership of Julius Nyerere.

African representation in the government was minimal, at best, but in 1926 some Africans were unofficially admitted into the Legislative Council (LEGCO) which was the colonial legislature or parliament.

In 1929, the Tanganyika Territory African Civil Service Association became the Tanganyika African Association which was eventually transformed into TANU in 1954. About 10 years earlier before TANU was formed, the first Africans were officially appointed by the governor of Tanganyika as members of the Legislative Council in 1945.

The transition from colonial rule to independence was a peaceful one under the leadership of TANU. Less than seven years after TANU was founded, Tanganyika became independent on 9 December 1961.

It was the first East African country to emerge from colonial rule under the leadership of Julius Nyerere who became prime minister. He was 39 and the youngest leader in the world during that time.

President Julius Nyerere, official portrait, 1965.

On 26 April 1964, Tanganyika united with Zanzibar to form Tanzania. It was the first union of independent states ever formed in Africa. And it is the only union of its kind that has ever been formed and which still exists today.

During his tenure as president of Tanzania, Nyerere became one of the most influential leaders in the history of post-colonial Africa. He was also one of the most prominent world leaders in the twentieth century despite the fact that his socialist policies failed to develop Tanzania.

But he had notable achievements in a number of areas in the domestic arena, especially in the provision of health services and education to the point where Tanzania had the highest literacy rate in Africa, over 91 percent; besides his highly commendable success as a champion of African liberation, especially in southern Africa when the countries in that region were under white minority rule. During his tenure as president, Tanzania was the headquarters of all the African liberation movements.

Chapter Two:

The Geography of Tanzania

TANZANIA is one of the largest countries in Africa in terms of area. It is - including the islands - about 380,000 square miles, bigger than Nigeria, the most populous country on the continent.

Tanzania also is one of the most populous countries in Africa. At this writing towards the end of 2006, it has a population of about 40 million people. And it stands out among all the other African countries because of its distinctive physical features.

These include the majestic snow-capped Mount Kilimanjaro which is also the highest in Africa; the three biggest lakes on the continent - Victoria also known by its African name Nyanza, Tanganyika, and Nyasa - shared with neighbouring countries; and the Great Rift Valley. The other high mountains are Mount Meru in northern Tanzania and Rungwe Mountain in the Southern Highlands.

In fact, it has the largest number of large lakes in Africa. Others are Lake Manyara, Lake Eyasi, and Lake

Rukwa besides the three Great Lakes of Victoria, Tanganyika, and Nyasa which is also known as Lake Malawi. But Lake Malawi is a controversial name since Tanzania also claims part of the lake despite Malawi's claim that no part of the lake lies within Tanzania's territorial boundaries.

And on the east is the Indian Ocean providing Tanzania with another body of water and an extensive coastline.

Coral reefs and mangrove swamps line the coast, a region also noted for coconuts. The coastline is lush and palm-fringed as are the islands of Zanzibar, Pemba and Mafia as well as other smaller islands in the Indian Ocean which are a part of Tanzania. Also the coastal regions are some of the most fertile parts of the country.

Grasslands and open woods in the interior dominate extensive plains famous worldwide for their wildlife.

The central plateau is a huge expanse of savannah and sparse woodland. It is largely arid and is the most infertile part of Tanzania besides some other areas of the country in the west and in the south.

Another distinctive feature of Tanzania is the large number of countries it shares borders with. It has the largest number of borders together with the Democratic Republic of Congo. Congo shares borders with nine countries and Tanzania with eight. The Indian Ocean is Tanzania's ninth border.

Tanzania is bordered on the north by Kenya and Uganda; Rwanda and Burundi on the northwest; Congo on the west; Zambia and Malawi on the southwest; Mozambique on the south, and by the Indian Ocean on the east.

The country can be described as having three geographical zones. The lowlands in the coastal regions; a vast, largely infertile plateau with an average of 4,000 feet bisected from north to south by the Great Rift Valley; and the fertile mountainous regions mostly on the margins of the plateau. Some of the most fertile parts are in border regions: around Mount Kilimanjaro in the northeast on the border with Kenya; in the northwest on the borders with Uganda and Rwanda; and in the Southern Highlands parts of which are on the borders with Malawi and Zambia.

Apart from the well-known mountains of Kilimanjaro and Meru in the northeast, and Mount Rungwe in the southwest, there are significant mountain ranges in Tanzania which are also some of the most fertile parts in the country. They are the Usambara mountains in the northeast; the Nguru and Uluguru mountains in the east; Livingstone mountains and the Kipengere Range in the southwest near Lake Nyasa; the mountain ranges surrounding Rungwe district also in the southwest; and the Ufipa highlands in the west near the southern part of Lake Tanganyika.

In addition to the major and smaller lakes, Tanzania also has fairly large rivers such as River Kagera in the northwest flowing into Lake Victoria; the Pangani River in the east which flows into the Indian Ocean; the Rufiji River in the eastern part of the country also flowing into the Indian Ocean; Ruvuma River which forms the border with Mozambique and also empties into the Indian Ocean; the Malagarasi River in western Tanzania which flows into Lake Tanganyika; and Kiwira River in Rungwe District which flows into Lake Nyasa.

The Pangani and Rufiji Rivers are major sources of hydroelectricity in the country. And there are many other smaller rivers in different parts of the Tanzania, including the fairly large Kiwira River in Rungwe District with the potential to supply electricity to many parts of Mbeya Region which borders Malawi and Zambia.

The physical dimensions of Tanzania are also interesting, with the distance from north to south, and from east to west, being almost the same. The mainland is 740 miles from north to south, and 760 miles from east to west. And the coastline is 500 miles long.

The total area of the country's lakes alone, more than

40,000 square miles, is more than three times the size of The Gambia, Africa's smallest country of about 11,000 square miles; and more than twice the entire area of Togo, another country in West Africa which is about 21,900 square miles.

Two of Tanzania's major lakes also have unique characteristics.

Lake Victoria is the largest lake in Africa, the largest tropical lake in the world, and one of the largest lakes in the world. It is 250 miles long at its greatest width and is relatively shallow. It has an average depth of 130 feet and a maximum of 262 feet. Some parts of the lake are said to be 375 feet deep but the maximum depth is usually considered to be less than that.

Lake Victoria has an area of 26,830 square miles and is the world's second largest freshwater lake after Lake Superior in North America. It also has the distinction of being the source of River Nile, the longest river in the world. The White Nile, the longest branch of the Nile River, flows out of Lake Victoria, while the other branch, the Blue Nile, originates from Lake Tana in Ethiopia.

Also there are more than 3,000 islands in Lake Victoria. The largest and most well-known is Ukerewe island which is part of Tanzania. And Ukerewe is another African name for Lake Victoria. The lake is critical to the well-being and livelihood of millions of people living in the surrounding districts in all the three East African countries of Kenya, Uganda and Tanzania.

Lake Tanganyika is the other one with distinctive features or unique characteristics. It is the longest and second deepest lake in the world. It is 420 miles long and more than one mile deep in the northern basin where it reaches 4,710 feet in depth. Its immense depth is attributed to the fact that it lies in the Great Rift Valley.

The deepest lake in the world is Lake Baikal in Russia. And by surface area, 12,700 square miles, Lake Tanganyika is the second largest in Africa after Lake

Victoria. But in terms of water volume, it is the second largest in the world after Lake Baikal in Russia. It holds a volume of water seven times that of Lake Victoria. And it is undoubtedly the deepest lake in Africa. And it has the largest volume of fresh water on the entire continent.

Lake Tanganyika also, which in some parts is 45 miles wide, plays a major role as a source of livelihood for the people of Tanzania, Congo, Burundi, and Zambia who live close to the lake. And together with Lake Nyasa, it has the largest variety of fish species not found anywhere else in the world. It is also known for its large populations of crocodiles and hippos and other forms of life. It is one of the most distinct natural habitats on earth. For example, about 98 percent of the lake's cychlids which comprise two thirds of the lake's fish are unique to Lake Tanganyika.

The third largest lake in Africa, Lake Nyasa which sometimes is called Lake Malawi especially by Malawians since the boundary dispute between Tanzania and Malawi has not yet been resolved, is the ninth largest in the world. It is 360 miles long and 25 miles wide. It has an area of about 8, 685 square miles and reaches depths of 2,300 feet.

Lake Nyasa also has the largest variety of indigenous species of cychlid fishes in the world. Researchers have so far identified more than 500 species which are not found in any other lake or anywhere else in the world. That is more than all the freshwater species found in all the rivers and lakes of Europe and North America.

Lake Nyasa also has another unusual characteristic. It does not have tides or currents. At the northern tip of lake Nyasa is Kyela district which was once a part of Rungwe District ringed by misty blue mountains.

Although Tanzania is a very large country, only about 5 percent of the land is used for agriculture. The reasons for such limited use of land are climatic and topographical. But there is a lot more arable land, about 10 percent of the total, which is used as pasture; and another 4 percent in the reserves which is suitable for cultivation.

About 23 percent of the land is allocated to reserves, the largest share of land resources allocated by any country in sub-Saharan Africa. The reserves include national parks such as the Serengeti; game reserves; and forest reserves.

Tanzania is divided into 26 administrative regions with about 130 different ethnic groups or tribes including racial minorities of Asian, Arab and European origin.

The regions are Arusha, Dar es Salaam, Dodoma, Iringa, Kagera, Kigoma, Kilimanjaro, Lindi, Manyara, Mara, Mbeya, Morogoro, Mtwara, Mwanza; Pemba North, and Pemba South, on Pemba island in the former island nation of Zanzibar; Pwani, Rukwa, Ruvuma, Shinyanga, Singida, Tabora, Tanga; Zanzibar Central/South, Zanzibar North, and Zanzibar Urban/West, on Zanzibar island which, together with Pemba island, once formed the island nation of Zanzibar.

The 26 regions are divided into 127 districts each headed by a district commissioner. And each of the regions is headed by a regional commissioner.

Arusha Region in the northeast on the border with Kenya is one of the country's most well-known regions because of its tourist attractions, geographical features and historical significance. They include the Ngorongoro crater in the western part of the region which attracts more than 200,000 visitors per year; the Serengeti national park most of which is in neighbouring Mara Region on the west also on the Kenyan border; and the remains of a 1,000-year-old stone structure at Engaruka in the Great Rift Valley, evidence of human settlement centuries ago.

Arusha Region also is home to Mount Meru, the second highest in Tanzania after Kilimanjaro.

Its capital Arusha is a well-known tourist centre. It is also the headquarters of the East African Community comprising Kenya, Uganda, and Tanzania; and possibly in the future also Rwanda and Burundi. And it is expected to be the capital of an East African federation if Kenya,

Uganda and Tanzania form a political union as they have said they intend to.

Omega, a Tanzanian woman from Arusha, who helped American students from Earlham College learn Kiswahili when they visited Tanzania in 2003.

Arusha was also chosen as the headquarters of the International Criminal Tribunal, a court set up by the United Nations to try cases involving the perpetrators of the 1994 Rwandan genocide for committing crimes against humanity. It is a thriving urban centre which has attracted many people from all parts of Tanzania and the neighbouring countries of Kenya and Uganda.

Arusha Region is divided into five districts: Arumeru,

26

Arusha, Karatu, Monduli, and Ngorongoro. Portions of the former Arusha Region districts of Babati, Hanang, Kiteto and a small piece of Monduli district were incorporated into a newly formed region, Manyara, which borders Arusha Region on the south.

The ethnic or tribal groups in the region are the Arusha, the Maasai, the Meru, the Mbulu, the Iraqw, the Rwa, the Mbugwe, and the Temi.

And not all of them are Bantu groups. Some are Cushitic, of Ethiopian origin, and others are Nilotic, originally from Sudan. And they have their own distinctive features, especially Cushitic groups, different from those of most Bantus. Even members of some Bantu groups have their own physical features which distinguish them from other Bantu groups.

Members of the Chaga tribe from neighbouring Kilimanjaro Region to the east are also found in significant numbers in Arusha Region, especially in Arusha town. It is the most cosmopolitan urban centre in Tanzania after Dar es Salaam, the former nation's capital and the largest city in the country which is also the commercial centre.

A member of the Zaramo, a Bantu ethnic group native to the coastal plains and low hills that surround Dar es Salaam.

Apart from being the largest city in Tanzania, Dar es Salaam also is the capital of Dar es Salaam Region. It is one of the smallest regions in terms of area, and the smallest on the mainland, but the most densely populated.

Almost the entire region is essentially an urban area because the city itself constitutes the region together with its surrounding areas. It is also the richest since the city of Dar es Salaam is the nation's commercial centre. It is also the nation's academic centre whose institutions of higher learning include the University of Dar es Salaam.

The city of Dar es Salaam has about 3 million people, which is almost the population of the entire metropolitan region. Officially, the nation's capital is Dodoma in central Tanzania but most of the government offices and most of the national government employees are still based in Dar es Salaam, as are most of the nation's leaders including the president of the United republic of Tanzania. Also all the diplomatic missions are still based in Dar es Salaam.

All of Tanzania's railways, although few, also originate from Dar es Salaam, including the Tanzania-Zambia Railway (Tazara) which goes all the way to South Africa. Dar es Salaam also is the country's main port on the coast of the Indian Ocean. And about half of the entire nation's manufacturing capacity is in Dar es Salaam although only about 10 percent of the country's population is concentrated in the city.

It is a thriving metropolis characterized by ethnic diversity among other things. All of Tanzania's ethnic groups including racial minorities (Arab, Asian and European) are represented in Dar es Salaam (popularly known as Dar). So are the country's religions. Like the rest of the country, the population of Christians and Moslems in Dar is roughly equal.

The region of Dar es Salaam is composed of three

districts: Kinondoni, Ilala, and Temeke, running from north to south in that order along the palm-fringed coast. The district of Ilala is considered to be the hub as a central district where most of the city is concentrated.

Kondoa District women carrying water.

The original inhabitants of Dar es Salaam, which was formerly known as Mzizima and as it is still called by some people, are the Zaramo and the Ndengereko, two of the country's ethnic or tribal groups out of a total of almost

130 mostly of Bantu stock.

But because of its cosmopolitan nature, mostly attributed to its status as the country's commercial centre and former nation's capital, the region of Dar es Salaam is now inhabited by people from all parts of the country and many parts of the world. It is virtually a microcosm of Tanzania's multi-ethnic composition and racial diversity. The new nation's capital Dodoma will probably acquire the same status in the future in terms of demographic composition.

Dodoma also is the capital of Dodoma Region. It is the twelfth largest region in terms of area and covers about 5 percent of the area of Tanzania mainland; that is, excluding the area of the former island nation of Zanzibar. Dodoma Region is in central Tanzania and is generally dry. But it produces millet and other grains; groundnuts, and tobacco in commercial quantities, as well as a variety of other crops including grapes. Livestock, especially cattle, are also a very important part of the region's economic well-being.

The region is divided into five districts: Dodoma Urban, Dodoma Rural, Kondoa, Mpwapwa, and Kongwa. Kongwa is also famous for the failed groundnut scheme in the late 1940s during British colonial rule. It was a scheme launched by the colonial government in an attempt to produce groundnuts in commercial quantities from large farms.

Kongwa also had the first school established by the British for European children in what was then colonial Tanganyika. The other European schools were Arusha, Lushoto, Mbeya, St. Joseph Convent in Dar es Salaam, and St. Michael's and St. George's in Iringa which was the premier school for white students in the whole country.

Iringa also is the name of one of Tanzania's 26 regions. Iringa Region is divided into seven districts: Iringa Urban, Iringa Rural, Kilolo, Ludewa, Makete, Mufindi, and Njombe. It has several tribes, including the Hehe indigenous to Iringa district, and the Bena indigenous to Njombe district, who are among Tanzania's largest ethnic groups.

The ethnic groups with more than one million people include the Chaga in Kilimanjaro Region, the Haya in Kagera Region, the Nyamwezi in Tabora Region, and the Sukuma in Shinyanga Region. The Sukuma are the largest ethnic group in Tanzania and are closely related to the Nyamwezi. The Nyakyusa in Mbeya Region are another ethnic group with more than one million people. They are indigenous to Rungwe district but are now the dominant group in two districts, Rungwe and Mbeya, in that region.

Other large ethnic groups or tribes include the Gogo (Wagogo) in Dodoma Region, the Ha (called Waha in Kiswahili) in Kigoma Region in western Tanzania, the Makonde and the Yao (Wayao) in Mtwara Region in the southern part of the country, and the Luguru in Morogoro Region. Other large groups or tribes include the Ngoni, the Nyika and the Maasai.

The "Wa" is a prefix used for the names of all the ethnic groups when identified in Kiswahili. Thus, the Chaga are called Wachaga, the Ngoni, Wangoni, the Nyakyusa, Wanyakyusa, the Nyamwezi, Wanyanwezi, the Sukuma, Wasukuma, the Haya, Wahaya, and so on.

The Haya or Wahaya are the largest ethnic group in Kagera Region which is located in northwestern Tanzania bordering Uganda, Rwanda and Burundi. Its capital is Bukoba, the second largest port after Mwanza on the shores of Lake Victoria. A large part of the region includes Lake Victoria. It is the 15th largest region in Tanzania and covers about 3 percent of the country's area.

Kagera Region has six districts: Biharamulo, Bukoba Urban, Bukoba Rural, Karagwe, Muleba, and Ngara.

The origin of its name has an interesting history. It was called the West Lake Region before it was named Kagera, and during colonial rule was a part of the Lake Province which included what is today Shinyanga Region and Mara

Region. It was renamed Kagera Region after the war between Tanzania and Idi Amin's forces which invaded the area and tried to annex it. In fact, in October 1978, Idi Amin announced that he had annexed 710 square miles of this northwestern region until his forces were expelled by Tanzanian troops.

The region is named after Kagera River which flows from Rwanda through northern Tanzania and into Lake Victoria. That is the largest river flowing into the lake and is therefore one of the sources of River Nile. It is, in fact, the most distant source of River Nile.

During the 1994 Rwandan genocide, thousands of bodies from Rwanda flowed down the Kagera River through Tanzania into Lake Victoria, sometimes more than a thousand per day. Some of the Hutu extremists who massacred the Tutsi said they were sending the bodies back to Ethiopia where the Tutsi supposedly came from, an act of ethnic cleansing reminiscent of the extermination of Jews in Nazi Germany under Hitler. The perpetrators of the Rwandan genocide massacred their victims five times faster than Hitler killed the Jews.

Southwest of Kagera Region is Kigoma Region which borders Burundi and the Democratic Republic of Congo. Lake Tanganyika forms an integral part of the region. The lake lies between Tanzania and Congo and is shared by the two countries as well as by Burundi on the northwestern tip and by Zambia in the southwest.

Kigoma Region is divided into four districts: Kasulu, Kibondo, Kigoma Urban, and Kigoma Rural. Besides Kagera Region, Burundi and the Democratic Republic of Congo, Kigoma Region also is bordered by Rukwa Region on the south, and by Shinyanga and Tabora Regions on the east. Undoubtedly, its most prominent feature is Lake Tanganyika, the world's longest and second deepest, just like another region, Kilimanjaro, stands out among all the regions in the country as the home of the continent's highest mountain.

Named after the majestic mountain, Kilimanjaro Region is mostly inhabited by the Chaga whose most important cash crop through the years has been coffee, despite its declining significance in recent years. Coffee has been one of Tanzania's major cash crops for decades and one its main foreign exchange earners grown mostly in Kilimanjaro Region especially in Moshi district; Rungwe district in Mbeya Region; and in Bukoba district in Kagera Region.

Coffee was introduced to Kilimanjaro Region by Catholic missionaries and went on to play a major role in the economic development of the region through the decades, as it did in Bukoba and Rungwe districts where it was also introduced by German missionaries during the same period.

Kilimanjaro Region is divided into six districts: Hai, Moshi Rural, Moshi Urban, Mwanga, Rombo, and Same.

It is one of the four regions of Tanzania bordering Kenya. Others are Arusha, Mara, and Tanga. Besides its border with Kenya to the north and east, Kilimanjaro Region also is bordered by the following regions in Tanzania itself: Tanga on the south, Manyara on the southwest, and by Arusha on the west. It is one of the smallest regions in Tanzania but also one of the most densely populated. And Mount Kilimanjaro is one of the biggest tourist attractions in Africa.

There are several other regions of Tanzania which share borders with neighbouring countries and the Indian Ocean. They include Lindi Region on the southeast coast. The regional capital is Lindi, a seaside town located on the Lukuledi River. Much of the region is in the Selous Game Reserve, one of the largest in the world. It is also the largest game reserve in Tanzania.

Lindi Region is divided into six districts: Kilwa, Lindi Rural, Lindi Urban, Liwale, Nachingwea, and Ruangwa.

Despite its great economic potential, it has the unenviable distinction of being one of the least developed regions in Tanzania. And the development of its port facilities in the town of Lindi has been overshadowed by the existence of larger and better facilities in Dar es Salaam, Tanga, and Mtwara which for years have served as the country's main harbours.

Manyara was, at this writing, Tanzania's newest region. It was a part of Arusha Region until 2002 when President Benjamin Mkapa announced the creation of this new region. Babati, a small town about 100 miles south of Arusha, is the regional capital. It is essentially a rural town and faced many challenges when it was designated as the region's capital, in addition to being the capital of Babati district.

Manyara Region is bordered by Arusha Region to the north; Kilimnjaro Region to the northeast; Tanga Region to the east; Dodoma Region to the south; Singida Region to the southwest; and by Shinyanga Region to the northwest. It also has one of Tanzania's main inland lakes and tourist attractions, Lake Manyara.

It is divided into five districts: Babati, Hanang, Kiteto, Mbulu, and Simanjiro.

The establishment of this new region, with Babati as the regional capital, drew some interesting comments from the district commissioner of Babati, Khadija Nyembo. She had this to say about the district's prospects and economic potential in an interview with the *Arusha Times*, April 12 - 18, 2003:

What are the main economic activities in Babati district?

Mainly agriculture. Farm produce, such as food and cash crops, are the major trading products in Babati.

Even food crops here are also earning us cash. For instance, traders from neighbouring districts and regions, always flock here to buy maize, beans and rice grown in Magugu.

Babati is the main source of food being used in Arusha, Kilimanjaro, Singida and even Dar es Salaam.

The district is also a rich source of animal products such as meat, milk and hides, another line of trade benefitting local livestock

34

keepers.

Are there any potential tourist attractions in Babati?

Oh! plenty. Tarangire National Park is in Babati, we also control a great portion of the Lake Manyara game park. Actually, all the hot and warm springs along and within the Lake Manyara basin, are in Babati district.

What about mining? The Emerald and Alexandrite quarries near Mayoka for instance.

Well, the quarries are within the Marang forest reserve which, apparently, is not exactly in Babati but part of Mbulu district. Despite the fact that the two gemstones are rare and very valuable, mining activities have been prohibited in the area because, as far as ecological experts are concerned, once allowed, mining activities would totally destroy both the forest environment and the area ecology.

This will in turn cause the forest to disappear and apparently it is the major source of rainfall for both Arusha and Manyara regions. Even Lake Manyara will dry up if the forest environment is tampered with.

So, which is the main source of income for the district?

That should be the collection of taxes in the district, but precisely development levy. We also collect hotel and bar taxes. However other forms of taxation such as crop produce, cattle and bicycle levies will soon be scrapped off as they cost a lot in collection but don't pay much. We also get annual subsistence funding from the central government.

What about tourism?

Tourism also contributes a lot in Babati district earnings, through the Community Development Initiative (CDI) in which National park authorities give out some monetary funding or material contributions towards development projects in the surrounding community or villages.

Again, as I pointed out earlier, big hotels are also major contributions in the istrict earning through hotel taxes.

How does the district benefit from Lake Babati?

The lake mostly benefits the local people who practise both fishing and irrigation farming in and around the lake. Fishing, however, is being done on a very small scale and is also being practised seasonally. We are currently also controlling fishing activities in a bid to conserve the lake.

Babati is now the headquarters of the new Manyara Region. Has this brought any changes to both the town and the district as whole?

There has been a great influx of people from other regions who, of late, have been migrating here to either try a new life or establish new business ventures.

With them, comes the usual trend of mass plot buying and land acquiring. So that we have to work twice as hard in sending out experts to conduct surveys in order to ensure that new, upcoming structures are built properly and according to plan.

Mushrooming buildings, especially on business premises, are also coming up at an alarming rate. Yes, the move to make Babati the regional headquarters has made the town experience rapid growth and increased population.

Even the previously closed down business ventures in town are in the process of being revived.

Now, with this influx of immigrants, how safe is Babati as far as crime is concerned?

Actually, it is not just a matter of immigrants, but the Babati crime scene has a long history of being part and parcel of the Arusha town criminal activities.

Crime here usually occurs at high levels during harvest time. This is when businessmen from other regions, especially from Arusha, come here to buy crop produce.

Robbers, of course, always tail these people knowing they are carrying plenty of money with them and in most cases they try to ambush them.

So, when robbery or theft cases occur here, it is usually by criminals from Arusha or even as far as Morogoro region.

Also, when criminals have committed crime in Arusha or anywhere near Babati, they sometimes try to come and hide here from the police.

Still, I very much commend the district police for their efforts in combating crime in Babati.

Much of the economic activities and revival the district commissioner talked about had to do with or could largely be attributed to the new economic policies adopted by Tanzania in pursuit of capitalism away from its socialist past.

Since the introduction of free market policies and

multiparty democracy in the early 1990s, which replaced socialism and one-party rule, many investors - local and foreign - have invested in the country making Tanzania's economy one of the fastest-growing in Africa; although the trickle-down economic theory has yet to be validated in the overall African context. The vast majority of the people, the masses, are still mired in poverty. And those in Tanzania are no exception.

Manyara Region, with its great agricultural potential and tourist attractions including Lake Manyara and Manyara National Park, has the potential to be one of the main beneficiaries from the nation's economic growth in this post-socialist era, although the negative impact of globalization on Third World countries like Tanzania can't be ignored or discounted.

Not far from Manyara Region, and located between Lake Victoria and the Kenyan-Tanzanian border is Mara Region which is also the home region of Tanzania's first president, Julius Nyerere. That is where he also was buried in his home village of Butiama a few miles from the southeastern shores of Lake Victoria after he died in October 1999.

Besides Kenya, Mara Region is also bordered by Mwanza and Shinyanga Regions on the south, and by Arusha Region on the southeast.

And although it is a small region, it has an impressive array of ethnic diversity. The tribal or ethnic groups in Mara Region include the Ikizu, Ikoma, Isenye, Jita, Kabwa, Kiroba, Kurya, Kwaya, Luo, Nata, Ngoreme, Ruri, Simbiti, Sizaki, Sukuma, Taturu also known as Datoga, and the Zanaki one of whose sons was President Nyerere.

That is far more than most regions have. Some of the biggest regions have fewer than that.

Mara Region is divided into five districts: Bunda, Musoma Rural, Musoma Urban, Tarime, and Serengeti.

During British colonial rule, Mara Region was part of

Lake Province around Lake Victoria together with Mwanza, Shinyanga, and Kagera Regions. After independence, Lake Province was renamed Lake Region in 1963. And years later, it was split into four smaller regions.

The world-famous Serengeti National Park is mostly in Mara Region. The park is famous for its annual migration of millions of white-bearded wildebeest also known as gnu. On the Kenyan side, sharing a common border with Serengeti, is another famous animal haven, the Masai Mara National Reserve. Within Tanzania itself, Serengeti is also bordered by the Ngorongoro National Park on the southeast.

Also close to Serengeti is the Olduvai Gorge where Dr. Louis S. B. Leakey and his wife Mary found fossil remains and artifacts of what many scientists and anthropologists believe to be evidence of the origin of mankind; an assertion disputed by the proponents of creation who contend that life is too complex to have evolved randomly without intelligent design.

One of the other border regions almost exactly opposite to Mara Region is Mbeya Region hundreds of miles in the southwest.

Mbeya Region shares a common border with two countries, Malawi and Zambia, on the south and southwest. And within Tanzania itself, it is bordered by Rukwa Region on the west; Tabora Region on the north; Singida Region on the northeast; and by Iringa Region on the east.

There are several tribal or ethnic groups in Mbeya Region. They include the Nyakyusa, the largest and dominant group of more than one million people which is also one of the largest in Tanzania; the Bungu, Kisi, Malila, Ndali, Nyamwanga, Nyiha, Safwa, Sangu, and the Vwanji or Wanji.

Some groups such as the Kukwe are considered by some people to be distinct ethnic groups but are really an integral part of some of the larger groups. For example, the Kukwe are basically Nyakyusa.

The Ndali are also closely related to the Nyakyusa. They speak basically the same language, use the same names and have the same culture but are considered by some linguists and anthropologists, such as Dr. Imani Swila of the University of Dar es Salaam who is a Ndali herself, to be a distinct ethnic group. The Kisi in Rungwe district, which is also the home district of the Nyakyusa, are another group that has been accorded status as a separate entity with its own identity distinct from the Nyakyusa.

Mbeya Region is one of the most fertile regions in Tanzania and is divided into eight districts: Chunya, Ileje, Kyela, Mbarali, Mbeya Rural, Mbeya Urban, Mbozi, and Rungwe which is the most densely populated in the region and one of the most densely populated in the country.

Some of the region's main cash crops include coffee and tea, mostly in Rungwe district where bananas also grow in abundance like in Kilimanjaro and Kagera Regions; rice in Kyela district, white potatoes in Mbeya district; maize, beans, groundnuts, sweet potatoes and vegetables in all the region's districts like in many other parts of Tanzania.

Mbeya, one of the largest towns in Tanzania, is the capital of Mbeya Region. In 2005, it had a population of about 300,000 people. It is surrounded by undulating hills and mountains and has a cool climate, often with cold temparatures in the morning and at night because of its high altitude of 1,700 metres.

Together with Iringa Region, Mbeya Region formed what was known as the Southern Highlands Province during British colonial rule. Today, the term Southern Highlands is still used but only as a geographical designation, with Mbeya Region being in the southwestern part of this area.

Mbeya Region, especially Rungwe district, enjoys

abundant rainfall, some of the highest in Africa and in the world. It is cool and misty much of the time and temperatures can drop to 32 degrees and below especially at high altitudes.

The Uporoto mountains in the northern part of Rungwe district have been described as some of the best yet least known for trekking in Africa. And the area around Mbeya town has been called "the Scotland of Africa." But botanically the vegetation on the hills is similar to that of the Western Cape Province of South Africa and less like what you find in the Highlands of Scotland. And Rungwe district also has the distinction of having one of the highest mountains in Tanzania and in East Africa: Rungwe mountain with an extinct or dormant volcano.

The Uporoto mountains and the Kipengere range surrounding Rungwe district are also the source of one of Tanzania's major rivers, Ruaha, which provides hydroelectricity to large parts of Tanzania. During the drought in 2005 and 2006, the government made attempts to save the water from Ruaha and other rivers in order to be able to generate enough electricity for the country. According to a report in the Tanzanian newspaper, *The Guardian*, March 21, 2006:

President Jakaya Kikwete has been asked to intervene and save Mtera and Kidatu dams by stopping encroachment on the catchment areas.

Good News for All Ministry, in a passionate appeal, requested for the President's personal intervention to ensure farmers and pastoralists are evicted from the dams catchment areas. The Ministry's head, Bishop Charles Gadi, made the call last weekend at Mtera during a three-hour prayer conducted at the dam.

His call came in the wake of a briefing by the Plant Manager, Nazir Kachwamba, and Operations Supervisor Akida Juma. The duo claimed much of the water flowing into Mtera dam was illegally tapped upstream for irrigation by farmers due to the ravaging drought.

The most affected areas include Pawaga, Kapunga, Madibira and Usangu wetland among others, they said. 'Mtera Power Plant is there for the national interest. If it is closed simply because there are some active irrigation schemes taking place along the catchment areas, the country may suffer economic setbacks due to lack of power,' said Bishop Gadi.

He also cautioned that if some farmers and livestock keepers were diverting water at the behest of some politician then the war against environmental degradation would be lost by the government. 'We know our president is a hard worker, through his philosophy of new speed, new vigour and new zeal, he will study this matter and rescue our dams,' said Gadi.

Earlier, engineer Kachwamba said Mtera Dam had never experienced such low levels of water (687.68m) down from the normal 698.5m in the past twenty years. This, he noted, had negatively impacted on the power production leading to the current power shedding in the country.

He said Great Ruaha and Kisigo rivers were the main water sources for Mtera Reserviour. He said the Great Ruaha has its source in the Uporoto Mountains and Kipengere Range in the south west of the Rufiji Basin. 'After entering the Usangu Plains the river passes through a number of irrigation schemes and then through an increasingly dry region on its way to Mtera,' he said.

The Rufiji basin that has just been mentioned is the largest in Tanzania and covers several regions including Morogoro and Pwani. Morogoro Region is separated from Mbeya Region by Iringa Region.

It was formerly a part of the Coast Province during colonial rule, and later of the Coast Region until the latter was split into three regions: Dar es Salaam, Morogoro and Pwani. Pwani means coast in Kiswahili.

The town of Morogoro is the capital of Morogoro Region. In 2005, the town had more than 200,000 people. It lies at the base of the Uluguru mountains and is the centre of agriculture in the region. Sokoine University of Agriculture is also based in the town of Morogoro which is about 120 miles from Tanzania's commercial centre and former capital Dar es Salaam.

Another major academic institution, Mzumbe University, is also in Morogoro, earning the region the distinction of being one of only two regions in Tanzania, at this writing, with more than one university. The only other region with this distinction is Dar es Salaam most of whose institutions of higher learning, mainly colleges and universities, are based in the city of Dar es Salaam itself.

Morogoro is a potentially rich agricultural region but it has now and then been ravaged by drought, destroying crops and livestock. The worst drought in many years was in 2005 and 2006 and it affected much of the country including other fertile regions such as Kilimanjaro. The drought also affected all the other East African countries of Kenya, Somalia, Ethiopia, Djibouti, and Eritrea.

Morogoro Region is divided into six districts: Kilombero known for its sugar plantations among many other crops; Kilosa, Morogoro Rural, Morogoro Urban, Mvomero, and Ulanga.

It is bordered by Tanga Region to the north; Pwani and Lindi Regions to the east; Ruvuma Region to the south; and by Dodoma and Iringa Regions to the west.

Another region not far from Morogoro is Mtwara which borders Mozambique. The two regions are separated by Lindi Region.

Mtwara Region has the unenviable distinction of being one of the least developed regions in Tanzania. But it also has the distinction of having played a major role in the liberation of Mozambique from Portuguese colonial rule during the liberation struggle in the sixties and seventies.

It was Mtwara which served as the rear base for the freedom fighters of FRELIMO - a Portuguese acronym for Front for the Liberation of Mozambique - when they were waging guerrilla warfare against the Portuguese army and colonial rulers in Mozambique. And it was Mtwara which had the largest number of refugees who had fled from Mozambique during the liberation war.

The region was bombed several times by the Portuguese in retaliation for the support Tanzania provided to FRELIMO, causing many deaths and inflicting heavy damage on the region. The refugee camps and innocent civilians in the villages were some of the primary targets of these attacks which included the use of napalm bombs.

The attacks by the Portuguese are one of the reasons why the region did not make significant progress in terms of development. But even without these incursions into Tanzania by the Portuguese, the region would still have lagged behind for other reasons, including poor infrastructure and lack of energy resources.

Even during colonial rule, whose infrastructure was inherited at independence, the region - which was then part of the Southern Province together with what is now Ruvuma Region and parts of Lindi Region - was virtually ignored by the colonial government and had one of the poorest road networks in the country.

But it has great potential for economic growth because of the resources it has. Mtwara, the region's capital, is one of Tanzania's three main harbours on the coast of the Indian Ocean, the others being Dar es Salaam and Tanga in that order, and to a much smaller extent, Lindi. Mtwara also serves as the gateway to neighbouring Mozambique and is the main port of call for ships and other vessels travelling from Tanzania to Mozambique and vice versa.

The exploitation of gas reserves at Mnazi Bay is also expected to play a major role in the development of the region by providing much-needed electricity. And there is some indication that the region may also have a substantial amount of oil, based on seismic tests and the discovery of some evidence for the existence of some petroleum reserves and other hydrocarbons in the coastal area, including oil seeps.

There is also some evidence that the region is gradually catching up with other parts of the country. Major roads and bridges have been built improving communication and transport facilities between Mtwara and neighbouring regions including Mozambique. They include a major road from the region's capital, Mtwara, to Dar es Salaam and a bridge across the Rufiji River, one of the three largest rivers in Tanzania.

The Rufiji delta contains the largest mangrove forest in the world. It is also believed to be the site of the ancient settlement of Rhapta, a trading post established centuries ago and mentioned in a first-century Greek booklet, *Periplus of the Erythraen Sea.* The settlement is said to have been built near the mouth of the Rufiji River. And evidence has been found showing that the people of the region conducted trade and other commercial activities with the ancient Romans for centuries.

The great economic potential of the Rufiji River and delta and its basin will undoubtedly have multiplier effect once fully harnessed, helping to fuel economic growth in the surrounding regions including Mtwara Region.

Mtwara Region is divided into five districts: Masasi, Mtwara Rural, Mtwara Urban, Newala, and Tandahimba. It is bordered by the Indian Ocean on the east; Lindi Region on the north; Ruvuma Region on the west; and by Mozambique on the south whose boundary with Tanzania is formed by the Ruvuma River, another reserviour of economic potential for the regions in southern Tanzania, especially Mtwara and Ruvuma both of which share a common border with Mozambique.

Mozambique is also linked with Tanzania by ethnic ties. Two major ethnic groups, the Yao and the Makonde, straddle the Tanzanian-Mozambican border with their lineage extending on both sides but having originated in Mozambique.

Also in 2002, the two countries formally agreed to build the Unity Bridge across Ruvuma River linking the two countries. It is expected to be completed in 2008.

At the opposite end is another border region with great economic potential and unique geographical features. This is Mwanza Region which together with Mara and Kagera Regions is on the shores of Lake Victoria in northern Tanzania where they were collectively known as Lake Province during British colonial rule. During that period, what is now Mwanza Region was simply Mwanza district,

44

just one among several in the Lake Province.

The mighty Lake Victoria is like no other on the continent in terms of size, a sprawling inland sea of majestic beauty, and not because it was named after Queen Victoria of England. Africans around the lake have always called it Nyanza, a great body of water, and source of sustenance for millions of them for centuries long before Europeans set foot on African soil, until one of these adventurers from Europe saw the lake and named it after the British Queen.

Mwanza Region on the shores of the lake is also home to Tanzania's second largest city, Mwanza, after which the region is named. The region also, together with Shinyanga Region, is the home of the Sukuma, Tanzania's largest ethnic group.

It is bordered by Kagera Region to the west; Shinyanga Region to the south; Mara Region to the east; and by Lake Victoria to the north some of whose waters are shared by Kenya and Uganda, the two countries bordering Tanzania in the northern part. Tanzania has the largest share of Lake Victoria, an entire half of the lake.

Mwanza Region is divided into eight districts: Geita, Ilemela, Kwimba, Magu, Misungwi, Nyamagana, Sengerema, and Ukerewe.

Besides the Sukuma, other ethnic or tribal groups in Mwanza Region include the Kara; the Kerewe indigenous to Ukerewe island in Lake Victoria; and the Zinza. And the residents of the city of Mwanza reflect the ethnic diversity typical of Tanzania in this multi-ethinic society, one of the most diverse on the continent.

Tanzania is one of the very few countries in Africa which have more than 100 tribes or ethnic groups; in fact fewer than five. The others are Nigeria, with more than 250; the Democratic Republic of Congo, with more than 200; and Cameroon with about 150. Tanzania has about 130, and they all probably have residents in Mwanza.

In 2005, the city of Mwanza had a population of about

400,000 people.

There is a lot of trade going on between Mwanza and the neighbouring countries of Uganda and Kenya across Lake Victoria. And the city is one of the main commercial centres in Tanzania. Industries including soap and textile manufacturing, fishing and meatpacking. The Mwanza Medical Research Centre conducting research in tropical diseases is also located in the city Mwanza.

In 1996, a national tragedy struck when a ship which had just left Mwanza on the way to Bukoba sank in Lake Victoria with more than 600 passengers aboard. They were mostly students going home for Christmas holidays and almost all of them died. Only a few were rescued by fishermen in boats and canoes.

Along the coast are five regions one of which is Pwani, literally meaning coast in Kiswahili.

Pwani Region is bordered by Tanga Region to the north; Dar es Salaam Region and the Indian Ocean to the east; Lindi Region to the south; and by Morogoro Region to the west.

It is divided into six districts. One of them is Bagamoyo. The district capital Bagamoyo is the oldest town in Tanzania. For centuries, it was the main slave trading centre on the mainland coast and point of departure for captured slaves bound for the Zanzibar slave market from where they were shipped to other countries including those in the Middle East. Some of them even ended up in the United States after slavery was abolished by the United States Congress in 1808 and anti-slavery patrols intensified on the West African coast to interdict ships carrying slaves, forcing the slave traders to turn their attention to East Africa, focusing on what is now Tanzania and Mozambique.

Besides Bagamoyo, the other districts which collectively constitute Pwani Region are Kibaha, Kisarawe, Mafia island, Mkuranga, and Rufiji.

Kibaha is the regional capital. It is also the capital of

the district after which it is named. The town is about 25 mile from the city of Dar es Salaam.

Mafia is the only district which is an island in Pwani Region. It is also a part of Tanzania's Spice Islands which include Zanzibar and Pemba. And it has many smaller islands around it, inhabited and uninhabited.

The island has a long history of foreign contacts dating back to the 700s AD. It played a major role in ancient trade between the Far East and what is mainland Tanzania today, especially the coastal area. And it was visited by Persian sea vessels on regular basis in the conduct of trade with the indigenous people including those from the mainland.

Some of these foreign merchants settled on Mafia island. Artifacts have been found confirming the existence of settlements by foreigners on the island - whose name has nothing to do with the Italian Mafia. It comes from the local language and the island has been known by that name for a long time even before the Cosa Nostra came into existence in Sicily in the late 1800s.

One of Mafia's smaller islands, the tiny island of Chole Mjini, had a settlement which was one of the most important towns in the conduct of trade from the silver mines of eastern Zimbabwe going through the old ports of Kilwa and Mikindani on the coast of what later became Tanzania.

It was also from Mafia island that the British first entered Tanganyika in 1914 during World War I, formally inaugurating their presence in the former German colony. In January 1915, British troops took over the island and used it as a launching pad for an aerial and sea assault against the Germans.

Almost exactly opposite to Pwani Region, hundreds of miles on the western border of Tanzania, is Rukwa Region whose capital is Sumbawanga which had more than 150,000 people in 2005. On the northern and northeastern parts it is bordered by Kigoma and Tabora Regions, respectively; by Mbeya Region on the east and southeast; Zambia on the south and southwest; and by Lake Tanganyika on the west which forms a border between Congo and Rukwa Region.

It is divided into four districts: Mpanda, Nkansi, Sumbawanga Rural, and Sumbawanga Urban.

The main ethnic group in Rukwa Region are the Fipa, a branch of the Ngoni who originally came from South Africa following disturbances known as *mfecane* in Natal Province during Shaka's reign. They were led by one of Shaka's former generals, Zwangendaba, and settled on the Fipa plateau in the 1830s, becoming one of Tanzania's ethnic groups.

The migration from South Africa covered more than 1,000 miles over a 20-year period. Zwangendaba died at Mapupo near Ufipa in 1848.

Some of the people he led from South Africa, from their original home near what is now Swaziland, moved further north towards Lake Victoria. Others crossed the border into Burundi and Congo. Yet others "retraced" their steps and went back south settling in what came to be known as Nyasaland and Northern Rhodesia, later renamed Malawi and Zambia, respectively.

Another branch which left Sumbawanga headed south wthin Tanganyika and settled in what is Songea today, named after one of the Ngoni leaders, Chief Songea, who chose to be hanged by the Germans during the Maji Maji uprising (1905 - 1907) rather than be allowed to go free, fearing that he would be considered a traitor by staying alive when many of his people had already died in the war against their German oppressors in what is now Ruvuma Region.

Ruvuma Region is one of the two regions which border Mozambique. The other one is Mtwara.

Songea is the capital of Ruvuma Region and Songea district. And it has a unique place in the history of Tanzania. It was in what is now Songea district where the bloodiest battles were fought by the Ngoni against the Germans during the Maji Maji war. It was also at Songea where they made their last stand, putting up stiff resistance against these alien intruders.

And it is in the town of Songea where there is a museum in commemoration of the gallant fighters who waged the Maji Maji war against the German colonial rulers in a campaign which is seen as part of the nationalist struggle against European conquest. It is the only museum of its kind in Tanzania.

Songea also is one of the largest towns in Tanzania. In 2005, it had a population of more than 130,000 people and is the region's main district since it is also the capital of Ruvuma Region.

Ruvuma Region is named after the Ruvuma River which forms the biggest part of the boundary between Tanzania and Mozambique. It is bordered to the north by Morogoro Region; by Lindi Region to the northeast; Mtwara Region to the east; and by Iringa Region to the northwest.

It is composed of five districts: Mbinga, Namtumbo, Tunduru, Songea Rural, and Songea Urban.

The Ngoni, whose home is Songea district, are the largest ethnic group in Ruvuma Region and one of the biggest in Tanzania. Others include the Matengo, the Ndendeule, and the Nyasa in Mbinga district.

Some of the main cash crops in the region are tobacco grown mostly in Songea district, and coffee and rice in Mbinga district. Maize, groundnuts, cassava, beans, vegetables and other crops are also grown in the region. Mangoes are also in abundance in and around Songea town. There are even mango trees in town, although not as many as in Brazzaville, capital of Congo-Brazzaville also known as Congo Republic, where some streets are lined by mango trees.

Not all parts of Ruvuma Region are fertile but significant parts are, making it a potentially rich region.

Also the people living along Lake Nyasa, especially the Nyasa in Mbinga district, derive sustenance and economic benefits from fishing in the lake, in addition to the crops they grow including rice, a staple diet in Tanzania.

Another region among the country's 26 regions is Shinyanga in northern Tanzania. It was once a part of the Lake Province during colonial times, and of the Lake Region after independence when the provinces were renamed regions in 1963, and is one of the two regions which are predominantly Sukuma. The other one is Mwanza Region.

It is bordered by Mwanza, Mara and Kagera Regions to the north; by Tabora Region to the south; Singida Region to the southeast; and by Arusha and Manyara Regions to the east.

Shinyanga Region is divided into eight districts: Bariadi, Bukombe, Kahama, Kishapu, Maswa, Meatu, Shinyanga Rural, and Shinyanga Urban.

Besides the Sukuma, the other two major ethnic groups are the Nyamwezi who are predominant in neighbouring Tabora Region, and the Sumbwa.

A variety of crops are grown in Shinyanga Region but the main ones are cotton, a major export crop; groundnuts, maize and rice mainly for local consumption.

The capital of Shinyanga Region is Shinyanga after which the region is named. It is also the capital of Shinyanga district which is famous for the production of diamonds at Mwadui.

Mwadui produces some of the best diamonds in the world, mostly industrial diamonds. And how they were found is an interesting story.

Canadian geologist John Thoburn Williamson, who earned a PhD in geology from McGill University in 1933, began prospecting for diamonds in 1936 in what was then called Tanganyika. But it was not Dr. Williamson who found the first diamond.

On 6 March 1940 in the morning when Dr. Williamson

was camped under a baobab tree during one of his attempts to find diamonds, his African helper handed him a pebble. Dr. Williamson held it up to the sun and immediately saw that it was a green diamond.

He also found out that he was standing on a Kimberlitic rock with the largest diamond mine ever found anywhere in the world. The oval-shaped volcanic pipe was filled with diamond-ferrous ore which covered about 361 acres on the surface, more than four times larger than any of the diamond pipes found in South Africa, then as now, the world's largest producer of diamonds.

Dr. Williamson named the site Mwadui, after the local chief, and it has been producing diamonds ever since.

It was one of the biggest discoveries in the history of mining anywhere in the world whose quest began in the mind of a young Canadian geologist in Canada, Dr. Williamson. He died of throat cancer in Tanganyika on 7 January 1958 just a few days before his 51st birthday and was buried in a cemetery at Mwadui.

The diamonds from Mwadui have made Shinyanga Region one of the major producers of gemstones and other minerals in Tanzania which are also some of the country's main export commodities and major foreign exchange earners.

Southeast of Shinyanga Region is Singida Region which was once an integral part of the Central Province before independence and of the Central Region after the end of colonial rule.

It is bordered by Shinyaga Region to the north; Manyara Region to the northeast; Dodoma Region to the east; Iringa Region to the southeast; Mbeya Region to the southwest; and by Tabora Region to the west.

And it is divided into four districts: Iramba, Manyoni, Singida Rural, and Singida Urban. Its capital is the town of Singida.

Singida is one of the poorest regions in Tanzania. It is a dry region like Dodoma, both of which were one province during British colonial rule, but enough crops are grown to enable the people to survive.

One of the main food crops grown in Singida Region is millet suitable for the harsh climate. Other crops include sorghum. And many people also earn their livelihood from livestock although this has been devastated by drought through the years as crops have been not only in Singida Region but other parts of the country as well.

The main tribal or ethnic groups in the region are the Gogo, the Nyiramba, and the Turu. And there are many people from other parts of Tanzania who are members of different tribes or ethnic groups living in the town of Singida which is also the capital of Singida district and the largest in the region.

West of Singida is Tabora Region most of whose inhabitants are the Nyamwezi, one of the largest ethnic groups in Tanzania.

Tabora is the regional capital. It had a population of about 130,000 in 2005 and was once the capital of the Western Province during British colonial rule. It was also an administrative centre during German colonial rule before the British took over Tanganyika.

One of the largest regions in Tanzania, it is bordered by Shinyanga Region on the north; Kigoma Region on the northwest; Rukwa Region on the west and southwest; and by Mbeya Region on the south.

It is divided into six districts: Igunga, Nzega, Sikonge, Tabora Urban, Urambo, and Uyui.

Tabora was also the home of one of Tanzania's most respected leaders, Chief Mirambo, who resisted Arab and German intrusion into his territory. And he is still a revered figure among the Nyamwezi even today.

Other Tanzanians also honour him as a national hero together with other traditional rulers such as Chief Mkwawa of the Hehe in Iringa Region as the predecessors of the modern nationalist movement which finally ended colonial rule. They were proto-nationalists who inspired others during their time. And many people even today still draw inspiration from them in defence of Tanzania and Africa as a whole.

The town of Tabora also had one of the first secondary schools in Tanzania, Tabora, which produced future national leaders including President Julius Nyerere.

It is also one of Tanzania's most important commercial centres, strategically located in a region which links western Tanzania with the central and northern regions around Lake Victoria. It is connected by rail with Dar es Salaam, the nation's commercial capital on the east coast; with Kigoma, a port town on the shores of Lake Tanganyika; and with Mwanza on the shores of Lake Victoria.

A number of important exports are traded in Tabora. They are also shipped from and through Tabora to Dar es Salaam and Mwanza for export and to other parts of the country for consumption. They include groundnuts, one of the main crops grown in Tabora Region; tobacco, another major crop in the region; livestock especially cattle; hides; cotton and other agricultural commodities. Honey also is one of the most important products in Tabora Region.

It is basically a dry region but gets sufficient rain for agriculture. One of Tanzania's largest rivers, Malagarasi, also originates from Tabora Region. And the area of Uvinza was one of the most important producers of salt for centuries and continued to play an important role in the production of this basic commodity even in recent times.

While the significance of Tabora as a major commercial centre has remained fairly consistent through the years, and may in fact even have risen, that has not been the case with Tanga which for decades was Tanzania's second largest town after Dar es Salaam.

Tanga's decline through the years, especially in recent times, has led to stunted economic growth of this once very important town which has also witnessed some changes in demographic patterns attributed to lack of economic opportunities, forcing a significant number of people to seek fortunes elsewhere in the country.

But its significance as one of Tanzania's largest towns remains. And it is the capital of Tanga Region which also has the distinction of being the home of what was once one of the most famous tropical research institutes in the world, the Amani Institute, built by the Germans when they were the colonial rulers of this vast country which they called *Deutsch Ostafrika*, and which included what is now Rwanda and Burundi.

Tanga Region is on the northeast coast of Tanzania. It is bordered by the Indian Ocean on the east; by Kenya on the north and northeast; Kilimanjaro Region on the northwest; Manyara Region on the west; Morogoro Region on the southwest; and by Pwani on the south.

It is divided into seven districts: Handeni, Kilindi, Korogwe, Lushoto, Muheza, Pangani, and Tanga.

In 2005, the town of Tanga had a population of about 250,000 people. Despite its size, it has been described as a quiet town in contrast with Arusha or Moshi in neighbouring regions, although all these towns are comparable in population size.

But it continues to play an important role as one of the main harbours on the east coast of Tanzania; the other two major ones being Dar es Salaam and Mtwara as we learnt earlier. Major exports shipped from Tanga include coffee, tea, cotton, and sisal which was once the largest export crop produced in Tanga Region.

In the past decades, the region had major sisal plantations and Tanzania was the largest producer of sisal in the world. However, its declining importance due to the introduction of synthetic material in the industrialized nations and low prices for the product on the world market are some of the major factors which have led to a reduction of investment in the production of sisal and forced many people out of work.

Yet, as a region, Tanga is one of the most fertile parts

of Tanzania and plays an important role in the production of cash crops such as coffee and tea. The Usambara mountains in Lushoto district are an economic power house for the region, not only in the production of tea and coffee but also as a tourist attraction. They have been called the "Switzerland of Tanzania," and sometimes of Africa. But probably the best or appropriate way to put it would be to say the Swiss mountains are the Usambara mountains of Switzerland, if not of Europe.

Although Tanga is no longer what it once was as a thriving coastal town, it is still an important urban centre in more than one way. It is a tourist attraction, serving many tourists who go there to see historical sites in the region and enter the world-famous Amboni caves.

It is also a major railway terminus connecting much of northeastern Tanzania with the sea and the rest of the country. It is linked by railway with what is called the Central Line, the major railway traversing a vast expanse of territory from Dar es Salaam on the coast of the Indian Ocean to Kigoma on the shores of Lake Tanganyika. The Central Line also branches out to Mwanza on the shores of Lake Victoria from west-central Tanzania. It is also linked with Tazara, another major railway which runs from Dar es Salaam all the way to Zambia and South Africa.

Tanga was also a battleground between the Germans and the Allied forces during World War I and became world-famous for what came to be known as the Battle of Tanga which is well-documented in history books. It was also nicknamed the Battle of the Bees because of attacks by swarms of bees during the battle.

The British launched an amphibious assault on the town of Tanga on 3 November 1914 in an attempt to capture German East Africa. It was the first major battle of the war in Africa. But it was a miscalculation and a disaster from the beginning, compounded by offensive and defensive tactics skillfully used by the Germans under General Paul von Lettow-Vorbeck who was, throughout the war, acknowledged by friends and foes alike as a master of bush warfare. The Germans were outnumbered eight to one yet won the Battle of Tanga. After the war, Von Lettow-Vorbeck returned to Germany as a decorated general and national hero.

We have, so far, looked at the regions on the mainland of Tanzania, 21 altogether. We now turn to Zanzibar or what was once the island nation of Zanzibar, now an integral part of the United Republic of Tanzania, which has five regions.

What was once called Zanzibar as a country has two major islands and several smaller ones. The major ones are Zanzibar, which is the biggest, and Pemba in the north close to Kenya. And both have administrative districts which constitute larger entities called regions under the union government of the United Republic of Tanzania.

Pemba island, the northernmost Tanzanian island in the Indian Ocean, is about 31 miles north of Zanzibar island and about the same distance from the Tanzania mainland. It had a population of about 300,000 people in 2005.

It has a higher elevation, more hills, than Zanzibar and it is more fertile. The main cash crop is cloves. But other crops are grown on the island, including coconuts. There are also strong indications that there may be some oil on and around the island, especially in the Indian Ocean.

The island does not have many tourists or other visitors but it has quite a reputation as a centre for traditional medicine and spiritual counseling based on African and Arab traditions. It also has more Arabs than Zanzibar island and has been an opposition stronghold since the introduction of multiparty politics in Tanzania in the early 1990s.

Tanzania's biggest opposition party, the Civic United Front (CUF), is strongest on Pemba island. In fact even numerically, most of the CUF supporters come from Pemba island. And opponents of the Civic United Front, especially on Zanzibar island, contend that the party wants

56

to restore Arab rule and break up the union of Tanganyika and Zanzibar.

The party also has a disproportionately high number of supporters who are Arab or of Arab origin. And because of this, it has always been swamped by the supporters of the ruling party, Chama Cha Mapinduzi (CCM) - which means the Party of the Revolution or the Revolutionary Party - in electoral contests on Zanzibar island who are predominantly black and apprehensive of the future should CUF win elections in the isles. They are afraid that the islands would go back to what they were before the 1964 revolution and would be dominated by Arabs.

The capital of Pemba island is Wete. The other important towns are Chake Chake and Mkoani. The island is also known as *Al Kuh Dra* in Arabic which means "the green island."

One of the interesting aspects of life on Pemba island are bullfights introduced by the Portuguese in the 1600s. They are still held in Pemba reminiscent of a tradition which conjures up images of bullfights in Portugal and Spain and of an era when the island was under Portuguese control.

The oldest ruins on Pemba island are at Ras Mkumbu, on the peninsula west of Chake Chake, where the Shirazis settled about 1200 AD.

The island has two regions: Pemba North and Pemba South. The capital of Pemba North is Wete which is also the capital of the whole island. The capital of Pemba South is Mkoani.

Pemba's sister island of Zanzibar is the largest island in Tanzania. It is about 25 miles from the mainland and was the scene of the 1964 Zanzibar revolution which took place in what was then the island nation's capital Zanzibar. The capitals of the former island nation and the island itself have the same name. It is the same town. The African name for Zanzibar island is Unguja.

The island's commercial centre is called Mji Mkongwe

in Kiswahili, which means Old Town. But it is usually called Stone Town in English. It is in the town of Zanzibar, the largest on the island and in the former island nation, and is the oldest part of this town. The architecture of the buildings in Old Town and in most parts of the town of Zanzibar itself as well as other parts of the island and in Pemba incorporates elements of Arab, Persian, Indian, European and African styles.

The site where Old Town is built has been inhabited for more than three centuries. Stone buildings were erected from the 1830s. It was the centre of trade, including the slave trade, on the East African coast between Africa and Asia before the advent of colonial rule, until it was eclipsed by Mombasa in Kenya after the 1800s. The main exports were spices including nutmeg, cinnamon, pepper but mostly cloves; and slaves until the Great Slave Market in Zanzibar was closed in 1873. Soon after the market was closed, the Cathedral Church of Christ was built on the site.

Stone Town became the launching pad for European penetration and exploration of the East African coastal regions and the interior and for colonial expansion into the mainland from the 1800s. Immigrant communities from Oman, Persia and India lived here, with Omani Arabs being the rulers of the island and the coastal areas of the mainland which were under the jurisdiction of the Arab sultan based in Zanzibar. The Omani rulers moved their capital from Muscat to Zanzibar in the 1830s. In 2005, the urban district of Zanzibar had more than 200,000 people.

The island of Zanzibar has attracted many people from different parts of the world through the centuries. The Sumerians, Assyrians, Egyptians, Phoenicians, Persians, Indians, Chinese, Portuguese, Arabs mostly from Oman, Turks, the Dutch, the French, the Germans, the British; they all have, at different times, lived on Zanzibar island for different periods of time in the island's long history of contact with foreigners, many of them hostile to the well-being of Africa, clearly demonstrated by their involvement in the diabolical traffic in human beings.

Even some American ships flying the Spanish flag went to Zanzibar to get slaves bound for the United States. The United also opened its first consulate in sub-Saharan Africa in Zanzibar in the 1830s and in 1835 Richard Waters was appointed the first US Consul.

The island has had a long history, much of it drenched in blood because of its participation in the enslavement of Africans by the Arabs for centuries. And its slave market was the last such market to be closed in Africa when the abolition of slavery went into full swing.

Yet, in spite of all this, Zanzibar has always generated a lot of interest in different parts of the world among scholars and laymen alike and people of all races round the globe.

Zanzibar is indeed an exciting and enchanting island, evoking images of a place of unsurpassed beauty in the minds of many people around the world; a place that is a tropical paradise in the placid blue waters of the Indian Ocean even if some of this may be more apparent than real.

But it is an exotic island, nonetheless, and with a rich and even if an inglorious past in some cases. As one Tanzanian agency, Bon Voyage Travel Centre, describes the island:

The very name Zanzibar evokes fragrant spices, Sinbad-the-Sailor look-alikes manning dhows with sun-bleached sails across one of the world's most historic water-fronts, sultans with harems of voluptuous women, veiled and clothed from head to ankles in black, and narrow alleys through which explorers marched and slaves were escorted to market.

All that, of course, has changed, though the dhows (mostly small now but otherwise much as they were) still ply the inshore waters and sometimes further. And though the sultans and their concubines, the slaves, explorers and British administrators have gone, their presence still lingers amid the old royal palaces, along the historic waterfront and among the high, closely-crowded Arab and Indian mansions, markets, shops, bazaars, mosques, cathedrals and one-time slave-markets of Zanzibar Island's Stone Town.

The women clad from head to toe in black still exist, and still wear the Islamic hijab (head-scarf) and bui-bui (Islamic gown). But few are veiled today and many wear scarves and gowns in colours other than black, often fashionably embroidered, though Islamic modesty and natural grace still prevail. Men also can often be seen in their traditional Muslim kofia (caps) and white kanzu (shifts), others wear smart but casual western-style clothes.

The best place to see all this living history, plus some important Arab and Indian architecture and ornate doors, and to get a real sense of Zanzibar's past - as well as its vibrant present - is in the old Stone Town, most of which would still be recognizable to David Livingstone, Henry Morton Stanley or even Sultan Said the Great. And the best way to see the Stone Town is on foot, with a good guide, all of which we can arrange.

But the Stone Town is only one of Zanzibar Island's many attractions. There are some beautiful near-white sand beaches, especially on the northern and eastern coasts, and little islands that you can visit by boat, and where you can swim and have lunch, or just relax by the sea. One island lodge, Chumbe, has won various international awards for its remarkable efforts to conserve Chumbe's marine environment, especially its coral reef, said to be one of the finest of its kind in the world.

Then there is Jozani Forest further south, home of the Zanzibar Red Colobus Monkey, found nowhere else, and perhaps of the rare Zanzibar Leopard, as well as other small mammals and many species of birds. Jozani is a natural forest full of interesting indigenous trees and other plants.

South of Jozani is the little fishing village of Kizimkazi, one of Zanzibar's oldest settlements with a lovely little 12th. century mosque which you can visit. Kizimkazi is also well-known for its dolphins, which you can usually see, or even join for a swim (though don't expect them to hang around waiting to be patted on the head!) just a short boat ride offshore.

Another enjoyable and informative way to pass a morning or afternoon on Unguja (as Zanzibar Island is known locally) is to take a "spice tour" to the island's celebrated spice-growing areas, north-east of Zanzibar Town. This is a "must" for any visitor, for Zanzibar without spices is like a zebras without stripes.

You will be astonished at the variety of aromatic spices and mouth-watering exotic fruits which you will see growing - and also taste if you take a tour which includes lunch. Such lunches are cooked outdoors, in an authentic village, by local women, and eaten sitting on the floor (as the sultans did, though they sat on the floor of a palace, not an open-sided thatched hut!) Nevertheless, the lunches are delicious and much recommended.

Spice tours usually incorporate a visit to one or more interesting ruins in the Zanzibari countryside, such as Marahubi Palace or the Persian Baths at Kidichi. Such ruins might be seen in several parts of Zanzibar Island, adding yet another touch of historical romance to this most fascinatingly exotic of islands.

For the more active and adventurous, Zanzibar has some of the best dive sites and snorkeling opportunities on Earth - or more accurately, under the sea.

Excursions and Main Places of Interest on Unguja (Zanzibar Island).

Stone Town and its vicinity

Largely nineteenth century Omani-style town with much Indian influence. Its architecture reflects these influences and various others, while the people you will see in its narrow lanes reflect Zanzibar Town's greater cosmopolitan nature, past and present.

In these streets sultans, slaves, soldiers and sailors once walked, famous Victorian explorers or administrators and veiled women passed each other in the bazaars, the women cloaked in black and in mystery, and perhaps trailing the scent of oud, the Arabic perfume.

But the Stone Town is more than a museum. There are good restaurants and hotels, internet cafes as well as souvenir shops, modern yachts and ships as well as dhows, stores selling electronic goods as well as markets dealing in sharks and swordfish, meat and vegetables and tropical fruits.

And the people in the Stone Town's narrow lanes now include holiday-makers from Italy, Japan, the United States and elsewhere, as well as business-people and locals.

Some of the main places of interest in Stone Town are listed below:

Sultan's Palace Museum

One of several royal palaces, this (and its predecessors on the same site) served as the "town house" of the Busaidi Sultans, looking out across the harbour. Part of a palace complex it was the main official residence within the Stone Town. The museum is furnished in what would have been typical nineteenth century style for members of the royal family. Sultan Said and some of his descendants lie buried in the palace graveyard.

Beit-Al-Ajaib (House of Wonders)

Designed by a marine architect (and looking a little like an upmarket oil rig), the Beit-Al-Ajaib was built as a ceremonial palace by Sultan Barghash. Spacious and airy and with some of the most beautiful carved doors in Zanzibar, it is now also a museum with many interesting exhibits.

Between it and the nearby harbour are public gardens where freshly barbecued lobsters, king prawns, varieties of fish, beef and chicken, eaten with delicious Zanzibari ajam (pancake-like bread) or the inevitable chips, can be bought and eaten in the evenings. You can "people watch" while you wait...

Site of Old Slave Market

The main Zanzibar slave market was closed in 1873 and soon afterwards the Cathedral Church of Christ was erected on the site, its altar directly above the place where slaves were once whipped for offending their masters. It is hard to imagine, in this now-peaceful place, the humiliations, and sometimes the horrors, that slaves must have suffered here.

The cathedral exterior has little architectural charm but its interior is inviting and interesting, with various items of historical interest.

Close to the site are the fish, meat and fruit-and-vegetable markets which can also be interesting if you can stomach the smell of fish and butchered meat.

Old Fort

Situated on the seafront, the fort is Portuguese in origin but owes much to later Omani reconstruction. There are craft shops inside and a café. Various exhibitions and shows are held in the fort's amphitheatre.

Livingstone House

Livingstone was invited to stay in this Arab-style house, overlooking the old dhow harbour, by Sultan Majid, while the missionary explorer prepared for what was to be his last expedition into the interior. He never passed through Zanzibar again except as a mummified corpse.

Old British and American Consulates

Situated by the sea in Shangani and once the temporary homes for various explorers (Stanley stayed at the American Consulate, now part of the Tembo Hotel). Livingstone's body once rested in a room, now an office, in the old British Consulate.

Tippu Tip's House

Also in Shangani, this old Arab-style mansion was the home of one of the best-known, most-feared Swahili slave-traders, a man who was often ruthless but also an adventurous and courageous traveller. Henry Morton Stanley among others had a grudging respect for Tippu Tip, and Livingstone himself was often supported by the very slave traders whose practices he loathed. The house itself is in poor shape but has a fine "Zanzibar" doorway.

John Sinclair's Architecture

Several buildings in Stone Town were designed by the British architect John Sinclair, who was enamoured of the Islamic style. Among his buildings are the State House, the High Courts, the Amani Peace Museum, the Old Post Office and the Bharmal Building.

Marahubi Palace

Ruins of Sultan Barghash's harem, just north of Stone Town. Barghash died before he could enjoy the delights of this harem and in any case it burned down soon afterwards. It must have been a most pleasant place by the sea, in attractive grounds shaded by mangoes and palms. Little is left but some old stone columns and a lily-covered pool where the women would perhaps have bathed, but there is a nostalgic, romantic and gently rural air about the place.

Mbweni Ruins

These ruins are in the grounds of the very pleasant Protea Mbweni Ruins Hotel, a little way south of Stone Town. They include the ruins of an old nineteenth century private Arab house, which was bought, transformed and extended to create a school for freed slave girls. Around them is a beautiful botanic garden.

Chumbe Island

Small island a short boat ride from Mbweni Ruins Hotel, lovely secluded place to spend a night or two. There is an old lighthouse on Chumbe but its main attraction nowadays is its award-winning lodge and the superb coral shelves which provide excellent snorkeling. Glass-bottomed boat also available for coral reef viewing. Rare and very large coconut crabs can be seen on the island.

Changu Island

A short boat ride from the Zanzibar waterfront, this small, wooded island was formerly known as Prison Island, though the prison, now in ruins, was never used. Pleasant little beach and nearby café. There are giant tortoises on Changu, brought from Aldabra, and in the woods tiny suni antelopes and several species of birds.

Beyond Stone Town

Places of interest in Unguja outside the town include Mangapwani Beach and Caves, a pleasant area north of Stone Town; Mtoni Palace, once the out-of-town home of Sultan Said but now in ruins; Dunga Palace; small ruined home of a local sheikh; Jozani Forest and Kizimkazi (both described in main Zanzibar introduction), and of course a huge number of wonderful beaches, mainly along the "Sunrise Coast" in the east.

Although slavery was formally abolished on the island, it continued thereafter, as did some other forms of involuntary servitude in which black Africans lived until the Arab monarchy was ousted from power in a bloody revolution in 1964. An estimated 20,000 people, mostly Arab, are believed to have been killed in the revolution, one of the bloodiest conflicts in modern African history.

After the revolution, many people, especially non-blacks, left the island nation. Some were expelled. These included Comorians from Comoro islands who themselves had been an integral part of Zanzibar for many years.

The island of Zanzibar is divided into three regions: Zanzibar Central/South with its capital at Koani; Zanzibar North whose regional capital is Mkokotoni; and Zanzibar Urban/West with the town of Zanzibar serving as the region's capital.

It is these regions, 21 on the mainland and 5 on the former island nation of Zanzibar, which collectively constitute the United Republic of Tanzania, the largest and most populous country in East Africa. As the population continues to grow, we should expect to have more regions carved out of the existing ones to facilitate administration even if that does not always mean decentralisation of government.

But devolution of power to the regions is something that we may expect in the coming years not only in Tanzania but also in other African countries as one of the best ways to serve the people by allowing them to make decisions at the local level on what is best for them in terms of development. It is also one of the best ways to defuse tensions and avert conflicts, most of which are generated and ignited by inequity of power, denial of justice, and inequitable allocation of resources.

As we continue our long journey into the twentieth-first century, we seem to be headed into a future in which some of the toughest decisions will have to do with how much power the people are allowed to have in order to determine their own destiny without undue interference from the central government, not only in Tanzania but in other African countries as well.

Chapter Three:

The People

THE demographic composition of Tanzania provides a unique perspective on the complexity of the ethnic diversity on the African continent, the second largest after Asia and with more than 1,000 ethnic and linguistic groups.

The linguistic diversity of Tanzania is unique in Africa. The majority of the people speak more than 100 Bantu languages in a country of about 130 ethnic groups indigenous to Africa. There are also some people who speak the rare Khoisan click language characterized by implosing consonants. It is spoken only by the Hadzapi and the Sandawi of central Tanzania in a country that is predominantly Bantu. But it is common among the so-called Bushmen and Hottentots of South Africa and the Kalahari desert in Botswana.

There are also speakers of Cushitic and Nilotic languages in central and north-east central Tanzania. These are Iraqw who speak a Cushitic language and who originally came from the southern highlands of Ethiopia about 2,000 years ago; and the Maasai who migrated from southern Sudan about 300 years and who speak a Nilotic language. There is another group, the Datoga, also called Mang'ati, who also speak a Nilotic language and are fierce fighters like the Maasai.

Maasai women

Then there are the Somali, originally from Somalia, who live in the coastal regions and other parts of Tanzania including a significant number of them in Arusha Region in the northeast and the north-central parts of the country.

There are also Tutsis and Hutus especially in the western and northwestern regions of Tanzania and in other parts of the country. Some were born in Tanzania. Others are refugees or descendants of refugees from the war-torn neighbouring countries of Rwanda and Burundi. In the early 1980s, tens of thousands of them were accorded citizenship by President Julius Nyerere. In 1980 alone, more than 80,000 Hutu and Tutsi refugees became citizens; beneficiaries of Nyerere's benevolent policies.

All these groups are indigenous to Africa.

Then there are the Arabs who constitute a significant part of the Tanzanian population especially in Zanzibar, Pemba, and along the coast. They originally came from the Arabian peninsula including the Gulf states more than 1,300 years ago and have lived in Tanzania longer than some ethnic groups indigenous to Africa have; for example, longer than the Ngoni who migrated to Tanzania from South Africa only in the 1830s, and the Maasai who came from Sudan about 300 years ago. Other groups from Mozambique also migrated to Tanzania a few hundred years ago.

An Arab trader in Zanzibar.

By some criterion, Arabs may be considered to be native to Africa because they have lived on the continent for so long, depending, of course, on how one defines the term "native." How long do people have to live in an area to be considered native to the region? What makes Bantu groups native to Tanzania and other parts of East and Southern Africa when there is historical, cultural, linguistic and archaeological evidence showing that they migrated from West Africa, especially from what is now eastern Nigeria and Cameroon, about 2,000 years ago? They were native to that region.

Whatever the case, Arabs are an integral part of the Tanzanian population and society and have contributed to the cultural vitality of the country and the East African region in a way other groups originally from outside Africa have not. It was from the interaction and intermingling between the Arabs and Africans along the coast for centuries since 700 A.D, and even before then, that East Africa saw the birth of a new society and culture along the coast of what is now Kenya and Tanzania and the islands of Pemba and Zanzibar.

It led to the birth and evolution of the Swahili language and the emergence of a virtually distinct ethnic group called Waswahili; a product of intermarriage between Arabs and Africans through the centuries. Arabs also have had a profound influence on Tanzania in another way through the introduction of Islam which became one of the major religions not only in Tanzania but in other parts of

Africa as well.

The name Swahili itself is derived from the Arabic word *sahil* which means "coast." And Swahili is the main language of the coastal people, Waswahili. It is also the national language of Tanzania and Kenya and one of the major African and world languages. It is also the only indigenous African language that is used as one of the official languages in the African Union (AU) together with English, French, Portuguese, and Arabic.

In spite of the Arab influence on the language, Swahili, which is usually known as Kiswahili among the native speakers, is considered to be an African language because its structure, syntax and grammar is African, and most of its vocabulary is African, derived from Bantu languages.

Only about 25 percent of the Swahili vocabulary is of Arab origin. There are also Persian, Hindi, Portuguese and English words in Kiswahili. It is also worth mentioning that Kiswahili is older than modern English and has written literature dating back to the 700s AD.

Every major international language has borrowed from other languages. And Kiswahili is one of them. Yet, by remarkable contrast, the English language has borrowed from foreign languages far more than Swahili has.

One Tanzanian scholar, Professor Deo Ngonyani at Michigan State University in the United States, posted on the Internet an answer to a question as to whether or not Swahili was really an African language. The question came from a post on August 11, 2005, on the Internet discussion group, "H-NET List for African History and Culture," in which the writer said the following:

I am familiar with the Kamusi Project and I think you are doing an excellent job. But I have a couple of questions about Swahili and its origin:

How did Swahili become the most popular African language in schools in the United States?
I don't think it has to do with the origin of African Americans.

Most of them came from West Africa probably even myself.

It is also the most well known African language among members of the general public in the African American community and many still learn it.

But many West Africans, at least the ones I know of, resent that. They say African Americans should learn West African languages. They also, together with others, contend that Swahili is not really an African language like Yoruba, Zulu, Xhosa, Kikuyu, Lingala or Igbo; it is mostly "Arabic." Is it? I think Professor Ali Mazrui says it's about 30
percent Arabic. Please correct me on that if I am wrong.

In his response to that, Professor Ngonyani who taught linguistics at Michigan State University had this to say:

I think that the popularity of Swahili (or Kiswahili, as the speakers of the language call it) is due to the fact that it is the most widely spoken African language south of the Sahara. And in East and Central Africa, it has become a pan-ethnic language. It has become widely used in education, media, and public discourse.

As for its Africanness, Swahili belongs to a group of languages known as Bantu. I spend much of my time studying the structure of words in different languages. I would like to share some of the salient features and put to rest some ideas that are not based on facts.

You can tell that Swahili is a Bantu language because, among other things:

(a) the word structure is typical Bantu: Noun classes and singular/plural prefixes, sometimes suffixes on roots that change other words into nouns; verbs are inflected for subject marker, tense, object marker, deriving new verbs with suffixes - all of these can be shown to belong to Bantu languages and in fact some very close relatives of Swahili in East Africa. (examples below)

(b) classification of nouns indicated by the prefixes

m-toto/wa-toto 'child/children'; ki-kombe/vi-kombe 'cup/cups'   jina/ma-ji
  m-tu/wa-tu 'person/persons'; ki-kapu/vi-kapu 'basket/baskets'   dirisha/ma
  (roots: -toto, -tu, -kombe, -kapu, -jina, -dirisha)
-all nouns are classified this way

Now compare how Arabic inflects the nouns using Roman alphabet - closer to its phonetics:

  jundub/janaadib 'locust/locusts' (root = j-n-d-b)
  nafs/nufuus 'soul/souls' (root = n-f-s)
  bank/bunuuk 'bank/banks' (root = b-n-k)

70

(c) a robust agreement system
ki-le ki-kombe ki-kubwa ki-mevunjika
that cup big is-broken
'that big cup is broken'

vi-le vi-kombe vi-kubwa vi-zuri vi-mevunjika
 those cups big beautiful are-broken
'those beautiful big cups are broken'

(d) a core of very common words which can be traced to Bantu   ancestry, and can

(e) phrase structure and sentence that is Bantu
etc.

Now compare Swahili and Arabic verbs:
Swahili
vi-me-vunj-ik-a
7-Tns-break-ST-FV (7-the class of the subject in the example above, -me- perfect tense, -ik- stative extension, -a indicative marker) Root -VUNJ-
'they are broken'

Arabic
zarara 'pull'
zarrara 'he caused to pull'
-the root for these forms is Z-R (or Z-R-R).

I could go on and on with many examples. But I will need only to note that Arabic does not share these salient features with Swahili. For example the word structure you find in Arabic dominated by three-consonant roots is not found in Swahili except for words that are conspicuously borrowed from Arabic. In Swahili, like other Bantu languages, you add a string of prefixes and suffixes. In Arabic, you insert pieces into the root as you can see in the examples.

While the Swahili word forms I have provided as examples are shared with Kikuyu, Zulu, Xhosa, Lingala, and other Bantu language, the Arabic word forms are shared with languages known as Semitic eg Hebrew, not with Swahili.

Therefore, in linguistic terms, Swahili is a Bantu language.

Having said that, I must note the heavy Arabic influence on Swahili vocabulary. That is clearly a result of contact with Arabic speakers, Islam, etc. This is the main reason people say Swahili is not an African language. Remember, a large percentage of Arabic words

71

in Swahili does not make Swahili and Arabic derivative. Every language borrows from other languages it comes in contact with. An example from perhaps the most studied language in the world (English) is going to be very informative.

In 1960s A.H. Roberts published results of his study of 10,000 most used English words. The study discovered that only a third of them were 'native' English words. That is to say only a third were of Germanic origin. About 60% were of Romance (Latin) origin (French, Latin). However, no one ever claims that English is a Romance language, or a sister to French, Italian, Spanish, etc.

Let me also add that Bantuists like Tom Hinnebusch and Derek Nurse have even identified Swahili's closest sisters on the Kenyan coast and have theories that suggest that is where its origin lies.

And as another Tanzanian scholar, Professor Frank Chiteji at Gettysburg College in Pennsylvania, stated during the same time in response to the same question on the same forum:

I think this question should be addressed to tanzlist(tanzlist@ccat.sas.upenn.edu), where we have some of the best minds on the language. I think of people like Prof. Lioba Moshi in Georgia, who has done a lot of work in this area.

I can only say that Swahili is perhaps one of the most widely spoken languages in Africa. It is estimated that more than 100 million Africans speak the language.

In my travels to Namibia, South Africa, Angola, Lesotho, Botswana, Swaziland, Mozambique, I have often ran into people who speak Swahili. People have called Swahili a trade language; I would to add that it is also a liberation language. Many of the echelons of the Southern African liberation movements speak Swahili.

Barbara Jean Palmer may also want to know that many of the top government officials in Southern Africa speak Swahili.

All of this is not to deny that other African languages are not important.

So, although Arabs had a profound impact on East Africa and continued to have significant influence through the centuries especially along the coast and in Zanzibar where they were the rulers; and in parts of the interior where they captured slaves; there is no question that they did not change or replace African languages with Arabic; and they did not fundamentally change the African way of life in a wider context even if they wanted to, except along the coast and in Zanzibar where they intermarried with Africans on a significant scale.

But even there, they did not totally replace African languages with Arabic. Instead, African languages fused with Arabic to produce the Swahili language which remained essentially African in grammar, structure and vocabulary because of the predominance of African languages and culture along the coast.

It is also worth remembering that Swahili is not only one of the major languages in the world - it is said to be one of the 12 major languages; it is also older than modern English. And there is no question that Arab influence on its evolution must be acknowledged as an integral part of Tanzanian history which includes the establishment of Arab communities in the coastal areas on the mainland and in Zanzibar.

Also along the coast and in Zanzibar were Persian settlers. They emigrated from Persia centuries ago and built settlements some of whose remnants still exist today. They originally came from Shiraz, in what is now Iran, and built some of the first city states in Africa along the east coast of Tanzania. They were founded by Persian princes who became the rulers of those city states the most famous of which was Kilwa on the southern coast of Tanzania. Its ruins still stand today as a monument to a bygone era.

The Persians also intermarried with Africans. In Zanzibar the Persians and Africans built a significant community whose descendants still exist today and identify themselves as Shirazis, although most of them are basically African. But a significant number of them do have Persian ancestry.

And even those who have only a little Persian ancestry still identify themselves as Shirazis. Some don't have any, yet they still call themselves Shirazis because of an inferiority complex. They are ashamed of their African heritage which they feel is inferior to anything foreign, regardless of how much some foreigners admire some aspects of African culture and way of life.

The Shirazi community in Zanzibar has had such a strong presence on the isles through the centuries that some of their descendants played a major role in the Zanzibar revolution of January 1964. So did some Arabs and others, and not just black Africans. In fact, the Shirazis and some indigenous Africans together formed the Afro-Shirazi Party (ASP) which spearheaded the Zanzibar revolution which overthrew the Arab sultanate and went on to form a union with Tanganyika which led to the establishment of the United Republic of Tanzania on 26 April 1964.

There were also Turkish immigrants who settled in Zanzibar centuries ago and became absorbed by the local population after losing dominance to the Arabs.

Greeks and Romans also came to Tanzania in ancient times long before the birth of Christ (BC). And coins and other artifacts have been found along the coast from that era and thereafter. Ancient Greek mariners called the coast Azania, what became an integral part of what is now Tanzania.

But it was the Arabs who lived along the coast the longest and left a lasting impact. However, their dominance was now and then interrupted by other foreigners in the same they conquered other people at different times.

The Persians, who were once dominant along the coast, were supplanted by the Arabs who in turn were conquered by the Portuguese. The Portuguese rose to dominance not only in the coastal area of the mainland but also on Zanzibar island. They conquered the Arab rulers in the 1500s and ruled the coastal area of what is now Tanzania for about 200 years until they were thrown out by the

Arabs in the 1700s.

But in spite of their 200-year dominance, the Portuguese left very little influence in the region besides the introduction of avocado from Brazil, as well as a few other things, and a few words like *mesa* which in Kiswahili is *meza* meaning table. Even today, when you travel around Tanzania, you hardly notice any Portuguese influence in the country. It is far surpassed by German and British influence in spite of the fact that the Germans ruled Tanganyika for less than 20 years, and the British for only 43 years.

The leader of Dawoodi Bohra community in Tanzania, Sheikh Tayabali Sheikh Hamza (L) and other High-ranking spiritual leaders of the community marching during celebrations to mark the 94th birthday of their leader, His Highness Dr. Syedna Muhammad Burhanud. From *The Guardian*, Dar es Salaam, Tanzania, Monday May 30th, 2005. It is a Muslim community founded in western India centuries ago.

The British, who ruled Tanganyika last, also constitute the largest community of European settlers in Tanzania. And there are many other Tanzanians of European origin, including recent immigrants. Also a significant number of whites from South Africa have moved to Tanzania since the end of apartheid. But they are mostly investors and it's not clear how many of them have become or are going to be Tanzanian citizens.

One community whose members have been in Tanzania longer than most Europeans, but for a shorter period than the Arabs in general, is the Asian community, mostly of Indian and Pakistani origin, but mostly Indian. It is also the most powerful and most influential among all Tanzanian ethnic groups in the economic arena.

Tanzanians of Asian origin have been influential in commerce since colonial times. There were immigrants who came from India centuries ago. But it was during the last 100 years or so that the majority of them settled in Tanzania. And they have remained a formidable force in the local economy and as merchants in the import-and export trade.

They constitute a significant community, although their number has declined through the years for various reasons, with many of them migrating to other countries, especially in the West. A number of black Tanzanians have followed the same migratory trend, mainly for economic reasons in search of greener pastures. But not all Tanzanians believe that grass is always greener on the other side. And they include Tanzanians of all races who have chosen to stay in Tanzania.

Although the vast majority of Tanzanians are Bantu, they differ in culture, customs and traditions, and in the way they earn their living even if there are no fundamental differences among them in many respects because of their common history and origin.

A few examples may help to illustrate this point, by no means typical of all the ethnic groups in terms of how they manage their lives and the degree to which the differences among them may be compared and contrasted with some accuracy. But the examples may still serve as a general guide and perspective from which we can try to understand the complex ethnic diversity that is typical of Tanzania.

The Maasai, sometimes known as the Masai, are probably the most well-known ethnic group in Tanzania who may even have inspired myths and legends about what they are and what they are not; similar to what some people have in mind about the Tutsi, for example conjuring up images of exotic Watutsi dancers to conform to the stereotypes, fact and fiction, about these African people in the Great Lakes region of East-Central Africa.

Even their origin is a subject of heated controversy and dispute even among some scholars and laymen alike, including the Tutsi themselves. There are people who say the Tutsi came from Ethiopia. Some say they came from the Horn of Africa. Others say they originated from Sudan or the area between Sudan and Ethiopia.

Yet others place their origin even farther, saying they came from North Africa. Kenyan Professor Michael Chege in the United States once mentioned a myth about the origin of the Tutsi in his article in an American journal *National Interest* in 1996 in which he said some people - they in fact accept it as a historical fact - say or believe that the Tutsi are the survivors of the lost civilization of Atlantis!

And to separate them from other Africans especially of Negroid stock, some Europeans including a number of scholars, call the Tutsi "black Caucasians," a term also applied to Ethiopians and Somalis in East Africa and to Fulanis in West Africa who are also said to have originated from Ethiopia like the Somalis and the Tutsi. All these people are also considered to be superior to Africans who are collectively identified as "Negroes" including Bantus.

Whatever the case, the Tutsi have been the subject of myths and legends through the years, just like a number of other African groups have been through the years, including the Maasai; although the origin of the Maasai, at least their recent origin in the East African context, is not in much dispute. They migrated from southern Sudan to

Kenya and Tanzania not too long ago as we learnt earlier.

And they are one of the major ethnic groups in Tanzania, a country of about 40 million people. They have also been the subject of great interest among foreigners and scholars because of their traditional way of life which has inspired studies and other scholarly projects even among fellow Africans in Tanzania and elsewhere. Tourists also like them.

Unlike most people in Tanzania who are predominantly of Bantu stock, the Maasai are pastoralists, covering vast expanses of territory in search of pasture for their livestock. They have followed their traditional way of life - as other Africans have - for centuries and don't even recognize the national boundary between Kenya and Tanzania, as they roam the land with their cattle; going wherever they have to go to find water and grass for their animals.

And this has sometimes led to conflict with some of their neighbours and others who are mostly farmers resenting such encroachment on their land. Just as pastoralists like the Maasai are worried about their cows, sedentary groups living around them or side-by-side with them are worried about their crops, and also about their land and water especially when it is scarce mainly during the dry season and when there is drought.

The closest relatives of the Maasai are the Turkana and the Kalenjin who live near Lake Turkana in west-central Kenya. And according to Maasai oral tradition and archaelogical evidence, they also migrated from that area. They are also related to the Samburu of Kenya.

And their defiance of the international border between Kenya and Tanzania in search of pasture has earned the Masaai in both countries quite a reputation as an independent people proud of their identity and traditional way of life before the coming of the Europeans who drew the boundaries and imposed new collective identities on Africans as Kenya, Tanganyikans, and so on. Their traditional grazing ground extends from central Kenya all the way to central Tanzania. They have also been glorified for their legendary prowess as the indisputable masters of the plains in that region.

More than anything else, cattle ownership is central to the economic well-being and identity of the Maasai. The cows are a symbol of wealth and status. They are rarely killed but are, instead, traded or sold. The Maasai often travel to towns and cities to buy the items they need and sell their cattle. And it is usually young Maasai men who are responsible for tending to the herds, living in small camps and moving constantly in search of water and pasture for their livestock.

And despite modernization and western influence, the Maasai have in most cases rigidly maintained their identity and traditional way of life, proud of their past and present.

The Maasai live mostly in northern Tanzania and in the central and northeastern parts of the country. Their neighbours include the Chaga, the Meru, and the Pare in northern and northeastern Tanzania; the Gogo in the central regions; the Sukuma in regions near Lake Victoria; and the Kaguru in central Tanzania.

A Kaguru in central Tanzania.

The Kaguru are Bantu but some of them look Nilotic or have Nilotic physical features, as shown in the picture here. And some of them may indeed be partly Nilotic. But the main reason many Bantu groups look different from each other is that the term Bantu is not a term of racial identity.

There is no such thing as a Bantu race. The term Bantu is a linguistic designation used only to collectively identify more than 200 African groups whose members speak related languages even if the people themselves are not closely related or are not related at all and have totally different cultures, traditions and life styles.

And they are all proud of their separate cultural identities just like the Maasai and other groups are, although many of them have been more susceptible to foreign influence than the Maasai have been.

Most Maasais are not only uncompromisingly pastoralist; they also have resisted any attempts - well-intentioned or not - to change their life style and be brought into the mainstream of modern life, which is really a euphemism for the western way of life and have in fact won respect for that even from many fellow Africans who ape western life styles and are dazzled by the glitter of western civilization.

The Maasai are immensely proud of their traditional way of life and their bodies painted in ochre, and when they are in their blue or red clothing, whether in front of tourists or not. In fact, their life style has been publicized worldwide for years. But it is probably not well-known that they obey strict dietary habits forbidding them for instance to consume milk and meat within the same day. They also observe the Cushitic taboo against eating fish, although they are not Cushitic but Nilotic.

Contrasted with the pastoralist way of life like that of the Maasai is sedentary living of people like the Nyakyusa, of whom I am one myself.

They are of Bantu stock and are native to Rungwe district in Mbeya Region in the southwestern part of the Southern Highlands. Their home district also provided them with security when their neighbours were being raided by stronger tribes such as the Ngoni and the Yao and by the Arabs, the latter two being involved in the slave trade which disrupted life and destabilized many parts of what became Tanganyika.

The Nyakyusa also had a reputation as fierce fighters. And they happened to have a homeland that was well-endowed in terms of food, climate and natural defence barriers surrounded by mountains.

And not only did they live in peace and relative prosperity in remarkable contrast with some of their neighbours; they were also excellent builders and farmers, using different advanced farming methods and techniques including terraced farming on the fertile hills of Rungwe district, irrigation, and building ridges and mounds of soil for planting crops, a fact also acknowledged by some foreigners including British historian Alison Smith who studied the Nyakyusa and wrote the following in a chapter

81

in the *History of East Africa Vol. I* (pp. 257 - 258):

> While there is every reason to believe that the lakeside scene (of Lake Nyasa) was in the early part of the nineteenth century one of relative peace and stability, it was shortly to be disrupted by Ngoni forays from the plateau to the west of the lake and by Yao slavers from the east.
>
> At its north-western corner, however, one enclave of people succeeded, almost to the end of this period, in defending themselves from attack, and remained little touched by outside influences of any kind up to the time when they came under the observation of the first European visitors.
>
> The kindred Ngonde and Nyakyusa people, distinct in origin from the Maravi folk, inhabited the pocket of superbly fertile country lying at the foot of the Kipengere Mountains; and while the Ngonde shared more or less in the effects of marauding by their more warlike neighbours, as well as being themselves early participants in the ivory trade, the Nyakyusa afford an outstanding example of the level of comfort to which, given a sufficiently favourable environment, African life could attain even within a simple Iron Age culture.
>
> Possibly it was this very degree of social consciousness and material well-being which, together with their numerical concentration and their remoteness, enabled them for long to repel attackers.
>
> The most distinctive feature of Nyakyusa society was the age-village, whereby male age-groups, together with wives and children, formed villages until the children became herd-boys and in turn hived off to form settlements of their own.
>
> They also had chiefs, who, unlike the mai body of the people, traced their origin to the (neighbouring) Kinga tribe - hunters and ironworkers - of the Livingstone Mountains in the east; and to these is attributed the introduction of cattle, which were the Nyakyusas' chief pride and care. They hung them with bells, and stalled them in cleanly byres, separate from their own dwellings.
>
> But they were also skilled agriculturalists, whose carefully ridged and manured plots climbed far up the valley slopes, planted with maize, yams, and sweet potatoes, but above all with bananas, the staples of their ample diet. The stability of an intensive cultivation, moreover, together with the need for protection from a heavy rainfall, caused them to be expert builders, and their conical huts, set about with banana groves from which the fallen leaves were swept daily, made an unforgettable impact on the African traveller.

One of those travellers was British explorer Joseph

Thomson who immortalized the Nyakyusa whose homeland and life style he described in one of the most famous passages in the history of African exploration. He first came across them in 1879 when he stumbled upon Nyakyusaland - which he described as "a perfect Arcadia" - and had the following to say in his book, *To the Central African Lakes and Back, 1881, Vol. 1* (p. 267):

It seemed a perfect Arcadia, about which idyllic poets have sung, though few have seen it realized. Imagine a magnificent grove of bananas, laden with bunches of fruit, each of which would form a man's load, growing on a perfectly level plain, from which all weeds, garbage, and things unsightly are carefully cleared away.

Dotted here and there are a number of immense shady sycamores, with branches each almost as large as a separate tree. At every few spaces are charmingly neat circular huts, with conical roofs, and walls hanging out all round with the clay worked prettily into rounded bricks, and daubed symmetrically with spots. The grass thatching is also very neat. The *tout ensemble* renders these huts worthy of a place in any nobleman's garden.

And as we saw earlier, Alison Smith briefly mentioned the age-group aspect of Nyakyusa society about which we are going to learn more for a better understanding of one of the largest Bantu tribes or ethnic groups in Tanzania.

The Nyakyusa did indeed have a unique life style through the decades and probably for centuries since they settled in Rungwe district about 500 years ago when they migrated from Mahenge in the eastern part of Tanzania close to the mighty Rufiji River. They are also a dominant group in neighbouring Mbeya district whose indigenes include the Safwa and the Sangu.

One of the largest ethnic groups with more than one million people, the Nyakyusa are one of the most studied ethnic groups in Africa. They first came to the attention of the academic world, at least on a large scale, through the writings of Professor Monica Wilson, a British anthropologist at the University of Cape Town who, with her husband Godfrey Wilson, studied the Nyakyusa in the

1930s and wrote extensively about them.

Until in the recent past, when the Wilsons were conducting research among them in the 1930s, the Nyakyusa had a unique life style based on age-villages, now largely abandoned with the encroachment of western civilization and other influences including modernization by Africans themselves.

The tradition of age-villages worked like this: From the age of 10 - 13, groups of boys would leave their parents' homes and villages and form their own new villages which would die at the death of the last survivor of the group.

The age-villages were the basic social units and building blocks of the Nyakyusa society. The villages were, and in many cases still are, compact in a highly densely populated district of Rungwe.

The age-villages were composed of well-built houses, fairly close together and usually along a broad, well kept village "street." As a general rule, the villages were composed of men who were around the same age, together with their wives and children. When the boys left home, as they were supposed and even required to by custom, they built huts adjacent to their parents' village and were still a part of that village although they had their own hamlet.

As they became adults, they started their own families. That was usually in their teens when they got married. In their early thirties or so, and in conjuntion with their coevals in similar hamlets attached to neighbouring villages, the young men established their own village and became independent of their parents. They were now free to conduct their own affairs, having attained political, economic and ritual autonomy.

The age-villages were not only an integral part of the Nyakyusa way of life; they incorporated and gave expression to certain fundamental Nyakyusa values such as cooperation, respect for elders, generosity, hospitality, dignity, wisdom, security and defence. The Nyakyusa believed that these values and virtues could best be learned and practised by people of roughly the same age, among peers, and by well-planned separation of the generations, children from parents, enabling and encouraging young boys to start early in life to be independent.

Nyakyusa girls

The Nyakyusa still cherish their traditional values and customs like other African groups do. But modernization has also had a significant impact on their traditional way of life especially since the introduction of western education, Christianity, and western ways of life which have spread across Africa, sometimes tearing up the social fabric of traditional African societies which held the people together and preserved their identities.

The identity of the Nyakyusa as an ethnic group has, like that of other African groups, been a subject of dispute among some scholars especially European and others who think and may be even apparently believe that they know more about Africans than Africans know about themselves. There is, for example, the argument that African tribes or ethnic groups did not even exist until the advent of colonial rule. They were created by Europeans or were a product of colonization.

The logical extension of this argument is that the Nyakyusa, the Igbo, the Shona, the Kikuyu, the Ganda, the Ewe, the Yoruba, the Maasai, the Bemba, the Zaramo, the Digo, the Chaga, the Pare, the Gogo, the Sukuma, the Nyamwezi, the Wolof, the Mandingo and all the other ethnic groups in different parts of Africa - not just in Tanzania - including their cultures and traditions, which are a concrete expression of peoples' identities, did not exist until Europeans came. Therefore even African languages, which are also distinct from each other and coincide with ethnic identity, did not exist until Europeans came. They all evolved under imperial rule, without which they would not exist.

That is the logic of imperialism, which includes cultural imperialism, few Africans subscribe to. As one African scholar, Walusako Mwalilino who is a Nyakyusa himself from Malawi and who also worked at the United Nations, stated in his article "In Defense of the Nyakyusa - Tanzanian People" in the January 1994 edition of an American publication *Monthly Review*:

The debate between Mahmood Mamdani and Basil Davidson in the *Monthly Review* of July-August 1993, which was sparked by Davidson's new book on Africa, *The Black Man's Burden*, requires an important correction. Both scholars present illuminating comments. My concern, however, is about one aspect only: the rectification of Nyakyusa history, of which both men seem to have insufficient understanding.

Davidson claims in his book that the Nyakyusa, who live in southwest Tanzania, as a tribe, were "invented" by European colonialism. He states:

'At first, the British set themselves to the work of inventing tribes for Africans to belong to; later, with possible independence looming ahead, they turned to building nation-states.'(1)

Among such formed "new tribes," he goes on, were: 'the Sukuma and the Nyakusa [sic], [who] rose fully formed from the mysterious workings of "tradition." Not being worried by such workings,

86

whatever Europeans supposed them to be, such coagulated clans and segments do not seem to have minded becoming "tribes"with exotic names. .but rather pleased about it.'(2)

While I cannot speak for the Sukuma because of my unfamiliarity with their history, the origins of the Nyakyusa do not jibe with Davidson's historiography at all. His mistake is based on John Iliffe's book, *A Modern History of Tanganyika*, which, on the subject of the creation of African tribes, Davidson lauds as "exemplary" and "excellent."(3) But what does Professor Iliffe say that Davidson finds so enlightening? The following passage represents the core of Iliffe's thesis:

'The most spectacular new tribe were the Nyakyusa. In the nineteenth century their name described only inhabitants of certain lakeshore chiefdoms. Some German observers and early British officials extended it to embrace also the Kukwe and Selya further north, their culture being broadly similar. After failing to impose paramounts on this essentially stateless people, the British established a council of chiefs in 1933 and described it as the tribal system. Buttressed by distinctive culture, common language, and sheer isolation, the newly-invented Nyakyusa tribe soon became an effective political unit.'(4)

In my opinion, this type of revisionist history is less than "exemplary" or "excellent." To start with, it's not true that in the nineteenth century the name Nyakyusa "described only inhabitants of certain lakeshore chiefdoms;" that they were a "stateless people;" or that they were an "invented" tribe. Let's consider the facts.

The heartland of the Nyakyusa is bordered by the Rungwe mountain in the north, the Songwe river in the south, and Lake Malawi in the east. Residents below the mountain, forty miles away from the lakeshore, also called themselves Nyakyusa. The whole area is now part of Mbeya Region, but the people still call their country Unyakyusa.

The Songwe river forms the Tanzania-Malawi boundary; a smaller number of Nyakyusa live on its south bank, inside Malawi. The Nyakyusa are closely related to the Ngonde, of north Malawi, who occupy the river's south bank and stretching forty-two miles south on the lake's plain.

The two groups speak the same language (with a minor difference in accents), although the Nyakyusa refer to their version as Kinyakyusa, while the Ngonde call theirs Kyangonde. And both groups pray to Kyala (God).(5) According to Malawian historian, Professor Owen Kalinga, the Nyakyusa settled in Rungwe valley between 1550 and 1650, a fact now supported by carbon dating.(6) The founders of the Ngonde nation settled in Malawi in 1600.(7)

Thus, centuries prior to the arrival of the British consul, Frederic Elton, in 1877, the first European to travel in Unyakyusa, the people had developed a political system of independent chiefdoms, without a central authority.

Elton negotiated with Nyakyusa chiefs to be given men--porters-- to carry his luggage en route to Zanzibar.(8) But what Elton didn't know then--and what Iliffe didn't know in 1979, and Davidson in 1992--is that the Nyakyusa, with their developed chiefdoms and sense of identity, had been living in Unyakyusa at least since 1650--a good two hundred years before their encounter with a white man!

Indeed, anthropologist Godfrey Wilson, who conducted field research in Unyakyusa from 1954 to 1958, has said as much: "The Nyakyusa, when the Europeans reached them, were organized in small independent chiefdoms."(9)

These chiefdoms were bonded together by their common history and Kinyakyusa language, and other cultural factors: rituals, customs, and conventions.(10) So the question arises: How could a people with this background have been "invented" by European colonialism?

Professor Iliffe is right, of course, to note that, "The common belief that colonialism imposed law and order on Africa needs always to be weighed against its tendency to disrupt the legal mechanisms of small societies.'(11) This certainly applies to the Nyakyusa, whose form of governance was severely altered by colonialism.

The destructive process was begun by the Germans who were the first to colonize Tanganyika (now the mainland of Tanzania) in 1895, nine years after the Berlin Conference allowed European nations to partition Africa. Their task of influencing the Nyakyusa directly, however, proved difficult because the Nyakyusa had a system of chiefs of equal standing; whereas the Germans wanted a paramount leader whom they could use as a conduit.

To overcome the problem, the Germans "introduced a paramount political authority among the Nyakyusa...in the persons of European officials."(12) The Nyakyusa bitterly resented this alien set-up, which led to their confrontation with the Germans on December 2, 1897. The Nyakyusa say "five hundred"of their men were machine-gunned to death that day; while Germans say they killed "thirty to fifty" men.(13) This massacre ensured German rule over the Nyakyusa for the next twenty-one years--that is, until 1918, when Germany was defeated in the First World War.

The British then took over Tanganyika, as mandated by the League of Nations, and introduced indirect rule among the Nyakyusa. They "created new Native Authorities under [a white] District

Commissioner and [who was] superior to the chiefs. The traditionally independent chiefs were grouped together in eleven court districts." (14)

But unlike the Germans, the British paid to newly-appointed higher chiefs. Iliffe quotes a paramount chief who, "shortly after his invention in 1926" (and here the word "invention" is quite appropriate), thanked British authorities in writing, saying, "You have given our country back to us." (15)

Iliffe somehow thinks this is how the Nyakyusa tribe was invented for the first time; he forgets that the newly invented chief had his own reason for thanking his new masters: he was on their payroll!

Iliffe further quotes a Nyakyusa person telling anthropologist Monica Wilson (wife of Godfrey Wilson): "Before you Europeans came,"--meaning, the British colonial administration--"the chiefs like Mwaipopo were not awe-inspiring, they feared the commoners very much .... It is you Europeans who have created chieftainship and awe."(16)

Again, Iliffe fails to realize that, implicit in the man's statement is the admission that prior to the coming of European colonial rule the Nyakyusa had a democratic system which did not allow for a big chasm between the chief and the commoners. A chief was easily accessible to the people; this eliminated the need for the people to be in awe of him. Only a corrupt or dictatorial chief had a founded reason to fear the commoners.

I also disagree flatly with Iliffe's assertion that the European "effort to create a Nyakyusa tribe was...honest and constructive."(17)

To repeat, the Nyakyusa tribe was not "invented" by European colonialism; rather, it was the victim of colonialism. The problem with Iliffe and Davidson, is this: they fail to make a distinction between the centuries-old origins of the Nyakyusa tribe and the imposition of new colonial institutions-- failure which leads them to confuse the two.

As for Professor Mamdani, he also makes the mistake--although not as serious as Davidson's---of gullibly accepting, in passing, Davidson's historiography about the Nyakyusa.

At no point in his long critique of Davidson's book does he question the author's accuracy about the Nyakyusa. Indeed, Mamdani's apparent lack of knowledge about the Nyakyusa is further revealed when he spells their name as "Nyakusa" (MR (*Monthly Review*), p. 39), thereby repeating the typographical error in Davidson's book (p. 100), from which he quotes.

In conclusion, the scholarship of Africa cannot truly advance if experts, no matter how liberal or progressive, take lightly--to say nothing of distorting, trivializing, or denigrating--the history of some African tribes, and particularly if those tribes are small and appear to be insignificant. The history of the Nyakyusa, although they are a small tribe, still deserves a better reading and interpretation.

Questioning the nature and identity, and even the origin, of African ethnic groups like the Nyakyusa may be a legitimate scholarly enquiry. But it is also an enquiry that has sometimes been compromised by shallow and biased scholarship. It can also sometimes complicate and even impede our understanding of the complexity and diversity of multiethnic societies such as Tanzania.

And when we look at the ethnic composition of Tanzania in an attempt to comprehend the scope of its diversity, we must also remember that the Bantu group or identity is virtually an arbitrary classification in terms of ethnicity.

In a way, it transcends ethnicity in the sense that it collectively defines or portrays as a monolithic whole all the different ethnic groups which constitute this family.

Yet it glosses over fundamental differences among them in terms of their unique or individual identities; for example, groups such as the Chaga, the Pare, the Arusha, the Meru and others whose physical features are suggestive or indicative of an identity similar to the identity of the people of Cushitic descent.

And there may indeed be some evidence of Cushitic elements or ancestry in some of these groups. Yet, they are all broadly classified as Bantu, giving a false impression that all or most of the members of the Bantu family - which is a linguistic family more than anything else - look alike.

But that is not true in all cases. The Arusha, the Chaga or the Meru don't, in general, look like the Makonde or the Yao or the Matumbi or the Kinga or the Safwa, and so on, although many of them do indeed look that way. But even if some of them do look like many of the members of the other ethnic groups which are identified as Bantu, there is still an underlying question as to why many of them also

90

look as if they are of Cushitic descent or some other origin.

A Meru woman

Such is the complexity and diversity of the demographic composition of Tanzania, unique on the entire continent. You have members of Bantu groups most of whose members are virtually indistinguishable from each other in terms of physical features.

But you also have Bantu groups whose members - at least many of them - don't look like "typical" Bantus but seem to be a people of Cushitic origin or of some other identity including Nilotic.

And you also have in Tanzania people who are indeed of Cushitic origin, the Iraqw and others. You also have Nilotic people like the Maasai. Then you have at least two ethnic groups, the Hadzapi and the Sandawi, who are not in any way fundamentally different from the people of the Kalahari desert, so-called Bushmen or Hottentots, derogatory terms used by Europeans to describe these people. All these are indigenous to Africa.

Then you have, of course, people of other races who originated from other continents, mostly from Asia and Europe, whose ancestors - especially of the Arabs - came to what is now Tanzania hundreds of years ago.

But it is the indigenous groups whose members constitute the overwhelming majority of the people of Tanzania, a formidable 98 percent, and whom we are going to look at further, because of their numerical preponderance, in order to get a comprehensive picture of Tanzania.

One of the most well-known of these groups are the Chaga. They are not only one of the most well-known Bantu groups; they are also one of the most well-known among all the groups in Tanzania.

They have more than 400 clans and live on the fertile slopes of the mighty snow-capped Mount Kilimanjaro. They are farmers who grow coffee, bananas and many other crops including beans, sweet potatoes, yams, and maize. And they have developed remarkable irrigation systems and advanced cultivation methods on terraced fields.

They were some of the first people in Tanganyika to get education provided by the missionaries, as were the Haya in Bukoba district in northwestern Tanzania, and the Nyakyusa in Rungwe district in the Southern Highlands. The Chaga also have a reputation of being businessmen and they are found in all parts of Tanzania in a country where ethnic cleavages and hostilities are virtually unheard of.

Another interesting group - they are all interesting, of course - are the Nyamwezi, their name meaning "the people of the moon." In fact, *mwezi* means moon and month in Kiswahili; also in other Bantu languages, for example, in my native Nyakyusa language - Kinyakyusa - in which we say *mwesi* for moon and month. Kinyakyusa is also one of the languages which does not have "hard" letters: z is replaced by s; r by l, v by f, and w by bw.

The Nyamwezi have a very interesting history, may be even unique in some respects. Native to Tabora district in western-central Tanzania, they were great traders and fighters and were the most powerful people in the interior, successfully challenging the Arabs' virtual commercial monopoly and power over Africans in the 1800s. They traded mostly in ivory, iron goods, salt and slaves and were famous throughout East Africa for long-distance porterage.

With an aristocracy and considerable slave population, their lives were regulated by secret societies with intricate initiation rites and gods who were worshipped, with the *mfumi* diviner wielding considerable power over almost the entire Nyamwezi population in Tabora district and beyond. They united in a vast confederacy of chiefdoms and various chiefs played a major role in the establishment of an extensive commercial empire unequalled during that period.

Those are just a few examples of Bantu groups. And we are going to provide more in this study, although the selection is arbitrary. No special criterion has been employed in selecting these groups. But they nonetheless serve as a microcosm of the larger Bantu family.

Looking at their life styles may shed some light on Bantu life in general because of the collective identity of Bantus as one people, in spite of some fundamental differences in different respects. But because we cannot look at all the ethnic groups in Tanzania in a comprehensive way, we have to select only a few out of about 130 for closer examination.

Among those examined here in more detail than others are the Luguru.

Also known as Ruguru or Waluguru, the Luguru live mostly in the Uluguru mountains in Morogoro Region in the eastern part of Tanzania and in the coastal plains near Dar es Salaam. They are one of Tanzania's largest ethnic groups with more than one million people and many of them are reluctant to leave their traditional strongholds in the Uluguru mountains because that is their traditional homeland.

They are mostly farmers and grow crops such as rice,

maize, beans, bananas, sweet potatoes, cassava, vegetables, sorghum and coffee. They also own livestock, mostly sheep and goats. They also raise poultry. Some of them are fishermen and wage earners working in towns and other places just members of other ethnic groups or tribes do.

Except during drought, the Uluguru mountains get abundant rainfall, making it possible for the Luguru to engage in intensive agriculture complemented by irrigation from streams flowing down the mountains. Some fertile parts can support up to 800 people per square mile. But they have no cattle because of tsetse-fly infestation.

Some of the largest sisal estates in Tanzania are in the lowlands surrounding Uluguruland. Besides Morogoro, the other region with the largest sisal estates in Tanzania is Tanga in the northeast.

One of the most well-known ethnic groups or tribes in Tanga Region are the Sambaa, also known as Shambaa, or Wasambaa. The neighbouring tribes are the Bondei and the Zigua, both in Tanga Region; as well as the Pare and the Chaga in Kilimanjaro Region which borders Tanga Region.

The Sambaa live in the Usambara mountains, some of the most fertile parts of Tanzania. They are related to the Zigua and they grow many crops in the fertile mountains. The crops include beans, maize, vegetables, bananas and other fruits and coffee. They are mostly farmers and plant various crops in terraced fields on the sides of the mountains where they live. Because of the fertile land they live on, and ample rainfall, they hardly experience hunger or famine. Not many places are so endowed.

One of the smallest tribes in Tanzania is the Kwere which had about 50,000 people in 2005 contrasted with the Sambaa, for example, who although not numerous had a population of about 200,000.

The Kwere live in east-central Tanzania near the coast and are bordered by the Luguru, the Zaramo, the Doe and other coastal people inclcuding the detribalized Swahili. They migrated from northern Mozambique into what is now Tanzania around 1000 AD.

They are mostly farmers like most Bantu groups are. The crops they grow include rice, maize, and millet. That is their staple diet. They also sell some of what they harvest.

Some of them own cattle, although they didn't in the past due to tsetse-fly infestation. Some of them are also fishermen although as farmers, traditionally, they usually trade with Swahili fishermen.

Because of the climate, the Kwere also grow or can get a variety of fruits and coconuts in these coastal areas. Among the cash crops they grow are cotton and tobacco.

Then there are other groups with their own interesting history. They are indigenous to Africa but they are not Bantu like the vast majority of Tanzanians.

There are three tribes in Tanzania which have a particularly ancient history. These are the Iraqw, the Sandawi, and the Hadazapi also known as the Tindiga.

The Iraqw in Mbulu district and surrounding areas with their distinctive features are the only tribe of Cushitic origin in the region. They became totally isolated from their original Cushitic cluster and have maintained their unique identity since then. They inhabited the Engaruka fields and evidence of human habitation around Lake Natron, Lake Manyara, and Lake Eyasi has been traced all the way back to the upper paleolithic period.

Traditionally, the Iraqw are agro-pastoralists. They operate a production system whereby manure produced by livestock is spread on the fields where it works as good fertilizer, while the livestock are fed on crop residues. Other tribes such as the Nyakyusa in the Southern Highlands of Tanzania also sometimes use cow dung as manure.

The main crops the Iraqw grow include maize, beans, wheat, barley, sorghum, sweet potatoes, white potatoes, peas and vegetables. Their main livestock are cattle, goats, sheep and pigs.

The Sandawi and the Hadzapi or the Tindiga are the oldest. The Sandawi who live in Kondoa district in central Tanzania originated from ancient tribes who lived in the area with the so-called Bushmen with whom they shared the Khoisan click language. But they are not, nowadays, as isolated as they were in the past and have been fairly assimilated.

Much of the assimilation has to do with the influence of their Bantu neighbours whose life style as farmers and herders and use of metal implements and weapons, including agricultural implements, has had a profound impact on the Sandawi. Some of them even speak Bantu languages because of this influence which has dramatically changed the Sandawi life style.

The traditional living patterns of the Sandawi left them isolated from their Bantu neighbours for centuries but were gradually pushed into the mainstream of the predominantly Bantu society which grew around them.

Even in modern times, they were largely isolated from the social and political mainstream and the government of Tanzania tried to discourage them from moving from place to place as they had done for centuries as their way of life. As a result, they lost their hunting areas; their sources of food diminished, and they found it very hard to make the transition to a sedentary way of life and take up farming. Their experience with farming and herding has been disastrous for them.

Traditionally, the Sandawi have been hunters and gatherers of food, moving their portable homes wherever they felt were suitable hunting grounds. And although the government of Tanzania has through the years encouraged them to adopt farming, many of them have resisted such intrusion into their traditional way of life.

However, a significant number of them have accepted modernization and about 25 percent of them have migrated to areas around Arusha in northern Tanzania and Dodoma in central Tanzania and other urban centres.

Many of them now own cattle and cultivate using metal hoes instead of their original digging sticks. But they still hunt. Among the animals they hunt include elephants besides deer, antelopes, pigs and other animals they value for meat.

By the way, the digging stick has also been used for generations by members of other tribes in Tanzania including the Nyakyusa in Rungwe district in the Southern Highlands. The stick the Nyakyusa use - it's V-shaped - is called *ngwabo* in Kinyakyusa, the Nyakyusa language, although it is now rarely used because of rapid modernization in most parts of Rungwe district.

The Nyakyusa have also been adept at using banana leaves as umbrellas and sometimes for covering roofs of their traditional homes in their home district where there is abundant rain, unlike in many parts of the country including central Tanzania where many Sandawis have lived traditionally. Again, this practice also has been largely abandoned in preference for better material including umbrellas and corrugated iron.

Besides hunting, Sandawi men also still collect wild honey while women gather wild fruits and vegetables and dig roots with sticks. And in spite of being a "primitive" diet, especially from a western perspective, the food the Sandawi eat is considered to be good and highly nutritious. And because of this, they are said to be much healthier than their Bantu neighbours. For example, they don't suffer from kwashiorkor or from many of the other debilitating diseases or conditions caused by nutrition deficiency prevalent among some of their Bantu neighbours.

And while they have basically maintained their life style, they have made some changes in the way they live including the way they build their houses. Instead of the traditional movable structures called *sundu* in their language, many of them now build more solid rectangular houses of the *tembe* type preferred by their Bantu neighbours.

Although some Sandawis have been converted to Islam and Christianity, especially Roman Catholicism, most of them still practice their traditional religion which includes reverence for the moon which they consider to be a symbol of life, fertility and goodwill. Their traditional beliefs emphasize cooperation and not confrontation with nature. Living in harmony with nature is also a common way of life among the San people of southern Africa who are related to them.

The Sandawi traditionally believe in a high God called *Warongwe* and they consider certain creatures - especially the praying mantis - and celestial bodies such as the sun, the moon, the morning star, and the southern cross as symbols of divinity. It is a strong faith among them which has also insulated many of them from foreign religious influences.

And despite repeated attempts at evangalization by missionaries, Christianity has not been very successful in penetrating and breaking down this "impenetrable" wall; nor has Islam. That is also one of the most important features of their life style which also sets them apart from their Bantu neighbours the majority of whom have accepted Christianity or Islam in a way the Sandawi have not.

As San people, related to the San of the Kalahari desert, the Sandwi are easily distinguished from their Bantu neighbours because of their different physical features. The Sandawi are smaller, have a lighter complexion and knotted hair like that of the so-called Bushmen of southern Africa who are their kith-and-kin. They also have the epicanthic fold of the eyelid like Orientals common to the San in the Kalahari desert.

The Sandawi language includes click sounds as consonants and is also tonal. It is not related to any of the languages around them. It is, instead, classified as a Khoisan language because it is related to the languages of the so-called Bushmen (San) and the so-called Hottentots (Khoi) of southern Africa.

And the Hadzapi - or the Tindiga - also in north-central Tanzania, are the only other aboriginal people in Tanzania who speak a Khoisan language. And they both - the Sandawi and the Hadzapi (Tindiga) - have provided a window into the distant past whose historical and archaelogical details have receded into the mists of antiquity.

By remarkable contrast, the Hadzapi or the Tindiga - unlike many of the Sandawi - still follow their ancient ways and are comfortable with their life style in spite of the hardship they face just to survive.

They are believed to be related to the pygmies (the Twa) of the Democratic Republic of Congo, Rwanda, Burundi and Cameroon but now speak Bantu languages and have more Bantu features because of the influence of their Bantu neighbours.

Twa is a Bantu name for the pygmies. And it is the same name the Zulu, a Bantu people, use for the Khoisan click-language speakers they found in their early migrations into what is now Kwazulu/Natal province of South Africa. One San tribe down there is still called Twa.

The Hadzapi - also known as the Hatsa - are still organized in the simplest form of society based on hunting and subsisting mainly on roots and fruits and animal hunting with bows and arrows during the dry season. They are believed to be the only remnants of the ancient paleolithic times on the entire African continent. And coincidentally or not, Tanzania itself is considered to be the cradle of mankind.

All that is testimony to the richly textured tapestry of Tanzania's ethnic diversity unparalleled on the continent.

Chapter Four:

Life in Tanzania

IT MAY BE an oversimplification to say that life in Tanzania is based on agriculture. But it is true.

The vast majority of the people live in villages in the rural areas where they work on the land, grow food and other crops including export commodities.

The urban population is small by comparison, although it is growing. For example, the population fo Dar es Salaam is about 3 million in a country of about 40 million people. That is 7.5 percent of the entire population of Tanzania living in Dar es Salaam alone, without even counting the people living in other towns and urban centres.

Still Tanzania remains, in all fundamental respects, essentially an agricultural country and will probably remain that way for many years to come.

A wide variety of food and cash crops are grown in different parts of the country depending on soil and climate. Some of the most fertile parts are in mountainous regions on the borders with other countries. Others include regions around the Lake Victoria and those along the coast.

The main food crops grown in Tanzania are maize, rice, pulses mainly beans; groundnuts, cashew nuts, bananas, plantains, mangoes, oranges and other fruits; wheat especially in Njombe district in the Southern Highlands; sweet potatoes, white potatoes, sorghum, millet, barley, cassava, cloves, cinnamon, pepper and other spices as well as many other crops. Some of them, for example cashew nuts and cloves, are major exports. Tanzania is one of the largest producers of cashew nuts in the world.

Fish are also available in abundance from the Indian Ocean, Lake Victoria, Lake Tanganyika, Lake Nyasa, from the country's several inland lakes and rivers. The fish are caught for local consumption and are also sold on the market.

Livestock are also a very important part of Tanzania's economy. Cattle, sheep, goats and pigs are the main ones. Chickens are also raised across the country providing meat and eggs for local consumption and for the market. Poultry and livestock are equally important in some parts of Tanzania, with some families owning poulty farms. But in general, individuals and families have only a few chickens per household.

The main cash or export crops are coffee, tea, cotton, tobacco, cashew nuts, pyrethrum, cloves and other spices; horticultural crops, oil seeds and others. Sisal is one of the exports although it is no longer the country's major export as it once was because of its replacement by synthetic fibres in the industrialized world.

Other export crops include coconuts and sugarcane. Grapes are also grown in Dodoma Region in central Tanzania for the production of wine.

Tanzania has a significant amount of minerals including gold, diamonds, nickel, tin, cobalt, phosphates, salt, gypsum, kaolin, and Tanzanite which is found only in Tanzania. But agriculture remains the backbone of the economy and the main foreign exchange earner. However, there are prospects that as mineral production continues to rise, mining is going to play an increasing role in the economic development of the country which at this writing was the third largest producer of gold after South Africa and Ghana.

Tanzania also has large quantities of coal and iron ore around Lake Nyasa in the South Highlands which have yet to be exploited. The country also has natural gas which is being used and there is a strong possibility that large quantities of oil also exist in the coastal areas and Tanzania's territorial waters in the Indian Ocean, especially around Pemba island and in Mtwara Region in southern Tanzania as well as in the Rufiji Delta.

The industrial sector is not well-developed but there are important industries which produce textiles, wood products, petroleum products, fertilizers, sugar, aluminium, cement, paper, steel, construction materials and other products. Cars and other vehicles are also assembled in the country although not on a significant scale.

By remarkable contrast, tourism is highly developed in Tanzania and is a major foreign exchange earner. Hundreds of thousands of tourists from different parts of the world visit Tanzania every year.

The agricultural sector has also attracted a significant number fo investors, including South Africans who have also invested in other sectors of the economy. White farmers from Zimbabwe have also sought investment opportunities in Tanzania.

Other major investors in Tanzania include Malaysians, Koreans and others from southeast Asia as well as other parts of the Asian continent including Indians, the Chinese and the Japanese; Canadians and Australians who have invested heavily in the mining sector; and the British who historically have been the biggest investors in Tanzania. There are also Americans who have invested in the country and people of other nationalities especially from Europe and Asia.

African investors in Tanzania, besides those from South Africa, include Kenyans and Ugandans. Also Ghana is one of the biggest investors in the mining industry in Tanzania, especially in gold mining.

The leading African country prospecting for oil in Tanzania is Algeria. A number of other countries are also involved in oil exploration in Tanzania which many analysts believe has not been fully explored in terms of mineral potential. Logistical problems, including harsh geography in terms of climate and physical barriers, are some of the biggest obstacles to economic development in Tanzania.

Tanzania is a large country, making it difficult to build an extensive road network and communication facilities; a problem that is compounded by the country's poverty. Only a few roads are paved and less than one percent of Tanzanians own cars. Buses are the major means of transport across the country, followed by trains.

In large towns including the commercial capital Dar es Salaam, transport is provided by taxis and mini-buses called *daladala*. In Dar es Salaam, city buses are also a major means of transport for people living in the city.

It is also in Dar es Salaam where the country's leading academic institutions are based. They include the University of Dar es Salaam, Tanzania's major university. There are also a number of other colleges and universities in other parts of the country.

There are also several newspapers published in Kiswahili and English, and a number of radio and television stations which broadcast in both languages. Most of them are based in Dar es Salaam.

In the area of education, Tanzania made tremendous progress under the leadership of President Nyerere unparalleled on the continent. It had the highest literacy rate in Africa and one of the highest in the world.

Education was free as were medical services under his leadership and everybody had access to those vital services. As Nyerere stated after he stepped down from the presidency when reflecting on Tanzania since independence, quoted in the London *Sunday Times*, October 3, 1999:

> We took over a country with 85 percent of its adults illiterate. The British ruled us for 43 years. When they left, there were two trained engineers and 12 doctors. When I stepped down there was 91 percent literacy and nearly every child was in school. We trained thousands of engineers, doctors, and teachers.

All that was achieved within 24 years. Tanzania won independence in December 1961. Nyerere stepped down in November 1985.

He also built a nation out of a diverse ethnic and racial population and achieved national unity unprecedented in the history of the continent; an achievement acknowledged even by some of his harshest critics. As the conservative *Wall Street Journal* conceded:

> Nyerere was a skilled nation builder. He fused Tanzania's 120 tribes into a cohesive state, preventing tribal conflicts like those plaguing so much of Africa.

Although Tanzania is one of only four African countries with more than 120 ethnic groups - others are Nigeria, Democratic republic of Congo (DRC) and Cameroon in that order - there is very little ethnic strife in the country. Most of them get along just fine, although tribalism has become more pronounced in some sectors since the introduction of multiparty politics in the early 1990s, with some politicians appealing to ethnoregional sentiments to advance their agendas.

Peace and stability in Tanzania is attributed to a number of factors: policies of cultural integration vigorously pursued since independence under the leadership of Nyerere transcending ethnic loyalties; promotion and use of Kiswahili as a national language; and the absence of a few dominant ethnic groups which would have been able to exercise control over others. Most of the tribes in Tanzania are relatively small, although the Sukuma are the largest with a few million people, followed by a few others with more than a million people each.

Tanzania also has significant numbers of racial minorities, mostly Indian, Arab and European, but race relations are generally good although members of different races, especially black Africans and the rest, don't mix and mingle as one would expect to see in a society where there are no serious racial problems. Racial tensions in Tanzania are rare.

Racial intermarriage has taken place through the years but mostly between Arabs and Africans in the coastal regions and in the isles - Pemba and Zanzibar - and in a lopsided way for racial reasons. For centuries Arab men married African women, had them as concubines, or simply slept with them because of the hegemonic control Arabs had over Africans especially during slavery.

It was unthinkable for black men to marry Arab women, although there were cases in which they had secret Arab partners. It is only in contemporary times that there have been a number of such marriages between black men and Arab women but also only in a few cases. Historically, marriage between Arab men and African women has been more accepted than marriage between black men and Arab women because blacks are considered by many if not by the majority of Arabs to be inferior to them.

In spite of such an asymmetrical relationship, relations between Africans and Arabs are generally good. Such amity, sometimes more apparent than real, can also be attributed to the fact that Arabs are no longer in a dominant position as they once were along the coast and in

Zanzibar when they subjugated and oppressed Africans.

In spite of the good race relations and peace and stability Tanzania is known for across the continent, and indeed in the whole world, there have been some incidents of racial animosity towards Tanzanians of Indian and Pakistani origin because of their dominant position in the economy more than anything else, fuelled by the rhetoric of racist politicians such as Reverend Christopher Mtikila, the leader of the Democratic Party, who in the late 1990s called for the expulsion of Asians and Arabs from Tanzania regardless of their citizenship status.

His highly inflammatory speeches led to some incidents of racial violence against Indian business owners in the commercial capital Dar es Salaam in 1998.

However, it is worth remembering that in spite of such attempts to inflame passions among black Tanzanians against Asians, Arabs and other non-blacks, the Democratic Party under Mtikila has not been able to win significant support among Tanzanians through the years. And prospects are bleak that it ever will if it continues to whip up racist sentiments against fellow Tanzanians of Asian and Arab origin and others who are - wrongly and sometimes for racist reasons as well -not considered to be African.

Yet it must be acknowledged that politicians like Christopher Mtikila and other agitators of his ilk are tapping into a reserviour of latent hostility among a significant number of black Tanzanians who resent the success of some of their fellow countrymen, especially those of Asian origin. Such hostility has led to the involuntary departure of a large number of Asian Tanzanians through the years, with many of them emigrating to western countries.

The former island nation of Zanzibar also has witnessed incidents of racial animosity between Africans and Arabs, although most of them have not flared into violence as happened during the Zanzibar revolution in

January 1964 in which thousands of Arabs were killed.

Yet, in a place which a history of violence even before the 1964 revolution, one cannot rule out racial violence in the future if whatever problems exist are not resolved amicably. Most blacks in Zanzibar - and this includes Pemba island - are apprehensive of the future should the main political party in the isles, the Civic United Front (CUF) which is supported by many Arabs, win elections. They believe that such a victory will lead to the restoration of Arab rule under which they suffered for centuries.

Another demographic trend which is gradually changing the country's landscape is the flow of investors and their families into Tanzania from different parts of the world since the introduction of capitalism after years of socialism which stunted economic growth and scared away foreigners who wanted to invest in the country.

The adoption of free-market policies has been one of the most significant changes in Tanzania since independence, especially in this era of globalization.

Some of the biggest investors in the country are South Africans who have been trekking north to this East African country since the end of apartheid. And they are destined to play a major role in the country's economic transformation for better or for worse.

They are also the most critical group of investors because of their proximity to Tanzania and their country's status as the economic power house on the African continent. As Mwalimu Julius Nyerere stated in one of his last speeches delivered impromptu and in an informal manner at the University of Dar es Salaam in December 1997:

South Africa, and I am talking about post-apartheid South Africa. Post-apartheid South Africa has the most developed and the most dynamic private sector on the continent. It is white, so what? So forget it is white. It is South African, dynamic, highly developed. If the investors of South Africa begin a new form of trekking, you *have* to accept it.

107

It will be ridiculous, absolutely ridiculous, for Africans to go out seeking investment from North America, from Japan, from Europe, from Russia, and then, when these investors come from South Africa to invest in your own country, you say, "a! a! These fellows now want to take over our economy" - this is nonsense.

You can't have it both ways. You want foreign investors or you don't want foreign investors. Now, the most available foreign investors for you are those from South Africa.

And let me tell you, when Europe think in terms of investing, they *might* go to South Africa. When North America think in terms of investing, they *might* go to South Africa. Even Asia, if they want to invest, the first country they may think of in Africa *may* be South Africa. So, if *your* South Africa is going to be *your* engine of development, accept the reality, accept the reality.

Don't accept this sovereignty, South Africa will reduce your sovereignty. What sovereignty do you have? Many of these debt-ridden countries in Africa now have no sovereignty, they've lost it. *Imekwenda* (It's gone). *Iko mikononi mwa IMF na World Bank* (It's in the hands of the IMF and the World Bank). *Unafikiri kuna sovereignty gani?* (What kind of sovereignty do you think there is?). So, southern Africa has an opportunity, southern Africa, the SADC group, *because* of South Africa.

Because South Africa now is no longer a destabiliser of the region, but a partner in development, southern Africa has a tremendous opportunity. But you need leadership, because if you get proper leadership there, within the next 10, 15 years, that region is going to be the ASEAN (Association of South-East Asian Nations) of Africa. And it is possible. But forget the protection of your sovereignties.

I believe the South Africans will be sensitive enough to know that if they are not careful, there is going to be this resentment of big brother, but that big brother, frankly, is not very big.

Although South Africa is not very big in comparison with the most developed countries in the world, it is the most developed in Africa. It is also the richest and the most powerful. And Tanzania is one of the African countries which have forged strong links with this economic giant on the continent to help develop some of the poorest and least developed countries in the world.

But the mere fact that South Africa is the continent's economic giant has generated an ambiguity among a number of Tanzanians of all races with regard to the role South Africans should play in Tanzania's economy.

Much of this ambivalence towards the South Africans in Tanzania can be attributed to the fact that although the country has achieved impressive economic growth almost every year since the adoption of free-market policies, the vast majority of Tanzanians have yet to enjoy the fruits of a liberalised economy. Little has trickled down to the masses; and the working class have to contend with loss of jobs because of privatisation, and with soaring prices of essential items including basic necessities they can't or can hardly afford.

Some of them, as well as others including university students, have even called for a return to the status quo ante of the socialist era when the Arusha Declaration imposed severe restrictions on the leaders to curb their predatory instincts and insatiable appetite for wealth accumulation at the expense of *wananchi*. Yet a significant number of them also shudder at such a prospect.

They may remember with nostalgia the good ol' days of socialism, depending on how one remembers those days, when egalitarian principles were implemented, giving the masses equal access to the country's wealth in terms of provision of essential services such as education and medical treatment which were free under Nyerere. But they also remember that they did not have the opportunity to earn money as they do now under capitalism which has enabled many of them to be self-employed, playing a vital role especially in the subterranean economy far more than they do in the formal sector.

Those are some of the major changes which have taken place in Tanzania since the early 1990s and which have transformed the social and political landscape of the country with little prospect that the nation will ever return to what it once was before during the socialist era of Nyerere. Much of that has to do with globalization, an irresistible force and whose terms are being dictated by the industrialized nations especially those in the West.

Although globalization is gradually - and even radically -transforming the face of Tanzania and the lives of many people in the country, the vast majority of Tanzania still live in abject poverty.

Most Tanzanians live in the rural areas basically the same way they have for decades. And many of those who live in towns earning wages have seen their living standards deteriorate due to loss of jobs and soaring living expenses, byproducts of a capitalist economy which has little concern for the weakest members of society.

Yet, it must also be conceded that a significant number of Tanzanians, especially those with high education and needed skills, have seen their living standards improve, sometimes remarkably, because of ample opportunities which exist in some sectors of the economy fuelled by free-market policies. And they are the least interested in supporting policies which will redistribute wealth to the poor at what they consider to be their expense.

So while a lot has changed since the end of the socialist era, to the vast majority of the people, life has remained basically the same because nothing has been done to alleviate their plight. They continue to live in poverty with little prospect for improvement in their lives.

The quest for regional integration is one of the ways the three East African countries of Kenya, Uganda and Tanzania hope will help to find solutions to regional problems and improve the living standards of their people. Whether or not that is indeed the case, and if the goal will ever be achieved, depends on the leadership and the kind of support the leaders get from their people in pursuit of this goal.

Included in this book are appendices on the East African Community (EAC) and on the prospects for an East African federation which has been an elusive goal since the first East African leaders - Jomo Kenyatta of Kenya, Milton Obote of Kenya and Julius Nyerere of what was then Tanganyika - agreed at a meeting in Nairobi, Kenya, in June 1963 to unite before the end of that year.

The federation was never consummated. We will have to wait and see if it is going to be, this time.

Appendix I:

The East African Community (EAC)

History and Background

The Permanent Tripartite Commission for East African Co-operation was first formed in 1967 as the East African Community. It collapsed in 1977 due to political differences. Following the dissolution of the organisation, former Member States negotiated a Mediation Agreement for the Division of Assets and Liabilities, which they signed in 1984. However, as one of the provisions of the Mediation Agreement, the three States agreed to explore areas of future co-operation and to make concrete arrangements for such co-operation.

Subsequent meetings of the three Heads of State led to the signing of the Agreement for the Establishment of the Permanent Tripartite Commission for East African Co-operation on November 30, 1993. Full East African Co-operation efforts began on March 14, 1996 when the Secretariat of the Permanent Tripartite Commission was launched at the Headquarters of the EAC in Arusha, Tanzania.

Considering the need to consolidate regional co-operation, the East African Heads of
State, at their second Summit in Arusha on 29 April 1997, directed the Permanent Tripartite Commission to start the process of upgrading the Agreement establishing the Permanent Tripartite Commission for East African Co-operation into a Treaty.

During a one-day summit in Arusha, Tanzania on 22 January 1999, the Heads of State of Tanzania, Kenya and Uganda resolved to sign the Treaty re-establishing the East African
Community (EAC) by the end of July 1999. The community was to take over from the Permanent Tripartite Commission for East African Co-operation.

In addition to a decision to re-establish the East African Community by the end of 1999, other issues raised at the EAC Summit of January 1999 included the signing of a Memorandum of Understanding on Foreign Policy Co-ordination; Zero tariff rates to be adopted by 1 July 1999 and the implementation of COMESA's 80% tariff reduction objective at the same time; setting up of a mechanism to deal with terrorism in the region; and postponement in admitting Rwanda and Burundi to the EAC.

Apparently, the inclusion in the agenda on the question whether Rwanda should be admitted to the EAC caused a heated debate during a preparatory meeting attended by the
three Foreign Ministers on 21 January 1999. The Ugandan delegation wanted Rwanda to be admitted, but Tanzania disagreed arguing that it was not possible to admit new members at this stage, as the procedure for doing so was still being debated. The proposal by Uganda was defeated when the Tanzanian and Kenyan delegates voted against it.

The Memorandum on Foreign Policy Co-ordination, signed by Foreign Ministers from the three countries, involves the three member states taking a common stand at international fora in assisting each other in countries where they do not have Missions. This entails that any of the three member states can appoint one Mission to represent their interests abroad. Nationals from the three countries will also be able to have visa applications processed in any of the Missions representing the region.

President Moi suggested that the countries of the region might even form a political federation and suggested in this regard the creation of a regional assembly with limited powers.

The East African passport was officially launched on 1 April 1999. At the same time, it was confirmed that the EAC planned to establish a free trade area in July 1999 and a common external tariff by the year 2000. In May 1999 a high level EAC task force met in Arusha and recommended a delay in the elimination of tariffs (to 1 July 2000) as well as a maximum common external tariff of 25%.

A meeting of experts took place at the EAC Secretariat in Arusha from 28 June to 7 July 1999 and resulted in the revision and redrafting of trade provisions of the draft treaty. Members of the three task forces also agreed on the creation of a customs union, the removal of internal tariffs by July 2000 and the removal of non-tariff barriers to importation of goods originating from the partner states within twelve months of coming into force of the treaty.

The Treaty for the Establishment of the East African Community was signed in Arusha on 30 November 1999. The Treaty entered into force on 7 July 2000 following the conclusion of the process of its ratification and deposit of the Instruments of Ratification with the Secretary General by all the three Partner States. The EAC was inaugurated in January 2001. The Treaty calls for a customs union (the framework of which was to be negotiated over the next four years), common market and monetary union and sets the ultimate objective as the birth of a political federation of east African states. Among the key institutions are an East African parliament, a regional stock exchange and a joint court of justice.

During the Summit of the Heads of State and Government, held in Arusha, Tanzania
on 2 March 2004, the presidents Mkapa of Tanzania, Museveni of Uganda and Kibaki of
Kenya signed a Protocol establishing the East African Customs Union. The Protocol will
have to be ratified by all three member states, and is expected to enter into force by 1July
2004. This will create a common market of 90 million people, with an estimated US$30
billion market potential.

Objectives

The Commission aims to improve and strengthen co-operation on the basis of the historical ties and understanding between the people of Kenya, Tanzania and Uganda. In this regard the countries emphasise co-operation in the priority areas of transport and communication, trade and industry, security, immigration and the promotion of investment in the region.

The EAC's bid to create a single East African market entails easing travel restrictions, harmonising tariffs, increasing co-operation among security forces, improving communications, sharing electrical power and addressing Lake Victoria issues. Concrete measures toward integration include freely exchangeable currencies (and ultimately a single currency), a common East African passport, a common flag and a double taxation accord. It also aims to abolish all tariffs with the aim of attaining economic and political   integration.

Each member would, however, be allowed to extract a maximum 10% surcharge on some products in order to protect indigenous industries, especially in the smaller economies of Tanzania and Uganda. This will be achieved through the establishment of a Customs Union as the entry point of the Community, a Common Market, subsequently a Monetary Union and ultimately a Political Federation of the East African States.

The regional organisation aims at achieving its goals and objectives through: -

• promotion of a sustainable growth and equitable development of the region,
including rational utilisation of the region's natural resources and protection of the
environment;
• strengthening and consolidation of the longstanding political, economic, social,
cultural and traditional ties and associations between the peoples of the region in
promoting a people-centred mutual development;
• enhancement and strengthening of participation of the private sector and civil
society;
• mainstreaming of gender in all its programmes and enhancement of the role of
women in development;
• promotion of good governance, including adherence to the principles of
democracy, rule of law, accountability, transparency, social justice, equal
opportunities and gender equality; and
• promotion of peace, security and stability within the region and good
neighbourliness among the Partner States.

The East African Community operates on the basis of a

five-year Development Strategy. The Strategy document spells out the policy guidelines, priority programmes and implementation schedules. The EAC strategy emphasises economic co-operation and development with a strong focus on the social dimension. The role of the private sector and civil society is considered as central and crucial to the regional integration and development in a veritable partnership with the public sector.

Establishment of an internationally competitive single market and investment area in East
Africa is accorded priority alongside the development of regional infrastructure, human
resource, science and technology.

Structure

The main organs of the EAC are the Summit of Heads of State and Government; the Council of Ministers; the Co-ordination Committee; Sectoral Committees; the East African Court of Justice, the East African Legislative Assembly; and the Secretariat.

The Summit consists of the Heads of State and Government of the Partner States. Its function is to give general direction and impetus to the achievement of the objectives of the Community. The Summit meets at least once a year to consider the annual progress reports and such other reports submitted to it by the Council of Ministers. It may also hold extraordinary meetings as necessary.

The Council of Ministers is the policy organ of the Community. It consists of the Ministers responsible for regional co-operation of each Partner State and such other Ministers of the Partner States as each Partner State shall determine. Among it functions, the Council promotes, monitors and keeps under constant review the implementation of the programmes of the Community and ensures the proper functioning of the regional organisation.

The Council meets in regular session twice a year, one of which is held immediately preceding a meeting of the Summit, and may hold extraordinary meetings as necessary. The Council may establish Sectoral Councils to deal with such matters as arise under the Treaty, and the decisions of such councils will have the same effect as those of the Council of Ministers.

The Co-ordination Committee consists of the Permanent Secretaries responsible for regional co-operation in each Partner State and such other Permanent Secretaries of the Partner States as each Partner State may determine. The Committee reports to the Council of Ministers and co-ordinates the activities of the Sectoral Committees.

Sectoral Committees report to the Co-ordination Committee. They are established by the Council on the basis of the recommendations of the Co-ordination Committee, that spell out their composition and functions. The Sectoral Committees prepare comprehensive implementation programmes, setting out priorities with respect to the various sectors as well as monitor their implementation.

The East African Court of Justice, initially, has jurisdiction over the interpretation and application of the Treaty on Common Market Matters. The Court's appellate, human rights and other jurisdiction are to be determined by the Council of Ministers in a Protocol to be concluded at a later date.

The East African Legislative Assembly is the legislative organ of the EAC. Its membership consists of 27 elected members, nine from each Partner State, plus five ex- officio members; the three Ministers responsible for regional co-operation, the Secretary General and the Counsel to the Community.

The Secretariat is the executive organ of the

Community. It is headed by the Secretary General who is assisted by two Deputy Secretaries General and includes the offices of Counsel to the Community and other officers appointed by the Council. The core budget of the EAC's Secretariat is funded by equal contributions from the Partner States. Regional Projects and Programmes are funded through the mobilisation of resources from both within and outside the region.

Autonomous Institutions of the Community are the East African Development Bank, Lake Victoria Fisheries Organisation, Inter-University Council for East Africa, East African Civil Aviation Academy, East African School of Librarianship; and such other institutions as may be established by the Council.

Peace and Security-Related Activities

Political and military tensions between the three economic powers of East Africa had long been strained by personal animosities between their leaders. Former President Moi of Kenya and President Museveni of Uganda were particularly mistrustful of each other, and Tanzania's brush with African socialism was a world apart from Kenya's pro-Western economic policies. However, these animosities are now mostly in the past, especially after the change of government in Kenya in 2003.

Although its priority is economic co-operation, the EAC believes it can play a role in
enhancing regional stability. In 1998, as a demonstration of the new spirit of co-operation, 1 500 soldiers from Kenya, Uganda and Tanzania took part in a joint training exercise in the desert terrain of Northern Kenya. The one-month exercise, code-named Natural Fire, was undertaken with assistance from the US Army.

A Memorandum of Understanding on Co-operation in Defence was signed in April 1998 and revised in 2001. On

18 October 1998, an EAC Summit on the security situation in the DRC took place in Nairobi. The summit agreed to support SADC efforts already under way in consultation with the UN and OAU.

The EAC has established a Sectoral Committee on Co-operation in Defence, as well as an Inter-State Security Committee. During 2003, these committees held meetings inter alia to exchange information on implementation of National Action Plans in line with the Nairobi Declaration on Small Arms and Light Weapons; to draft modalities for a common refugee registration mechanism; and a Defence Experts' Working Group on Operations and Training to discuss joint exercises on peacekeeping operations, counter-terrorism and military level participation in disaster response.

This profile was compiled by the Institute for Security Studies. Please send comments and /or corrections to: nico@iss.org.za.

In a major development in East Africa, Kenya, Uganda and Tanzania decided to join hands and form a trade bloc called East African Community (EAC) in January 2001. The new trade bloc aims to work towards economic policies that are pro-market, pro-private sector and pro-liberalisation.

By pooling in their resources and promoting free trade within the region, the East African Community aims to emerge as a leading trade entity in East Africa. In a simple ceremony held in Arusha, Tanzania, Kenya's President Daniel arap Moi, Uganda's Yoweri Museveni and Tanzania's Benjamin Mkapa, formalised the EAC treaty to pave way for an economic and, ultimately, political union of the three countries.

"Everything that we have done up to now has just been the preparation, the work for integration has just begun," Mkapa said at the official ceremony. "The important goals of the EAC are to improve our economies, quality of life and relations between the three countries," he said. Technocrats who have been working towards the cooperation have termed it "a new chapter" in which "none of the old mistakes will be repeated".

The "old mistakes" refer to the problems which led to the collapse of the EAC in 1977. East Africa had become ideologically split then, with Kenya advocating capitalism and social interventions, while Tanzania pursued socialism. Besides, mistrust among the leaders mounted especially after Uganda's former dictator Idi Amin took power by force.

Moi, Museveni and Mkapa had signed the treaty in November 1999 which set out the principles for economic, monetary and political union. It also provided for common action on the movement of people and goods between member countries and on transport, tourism and telecommunications. The treaty calls for common external tariffs and the elimination of international tariffs, the establishment of an East African legislative assembly and of a common customs union.

Rwandan President Paul Kagame and his Burundian counterpart, Pierre Buyoya, also expressed their desire to join the community. However, President Mkapa noted that their admission could only take place once the state of insecurity in their countries had been permanently addressed.

The East African region (Tanzania, Kenya and Uganda) covers an area of 1.8 million square kilometres with a combined population of about 80 million and has a vast potential in mineral, water, energy, forestry and wildlife resources. It also has agricultural, livestock, industry and tourism development. Its people have a common history, language (Kiswahili), culture and infrastructure. The EAC integration was aborted in 1977 after 10 years. Efforts to revive the community began in 1993 with the heads of state signing an agreement to establish a commission for East African cooperation.

United Nations Secretary-General Kofi Annan welcomed the creation of the new association, calling the newly established regional body a "building block" for a future African Economic Community.

"The United Nations supports the strong commitment of African countries to multilateralism and initiatives such as the EAC (East African Community) that strengthen Africa's capacity to meet the challenges of globalisation," he said.

However, the East African region has had its fair share of disputes and disagreements.

The main bone of contention has been the long-held perception by Uganda and Tanzania that Kenya's economy - mainly the manufacturing sector - was more competitive than theirs despite the fact that it has been declining over the past few years under pressure from imports from the Middle East and inadequate infrastructure.

Kenya exports approximately three-fifths of its goods to Uganda and Tanzania and had been facing tariffs of between 10 and 20 per cent before the establishment of the East African Community. However, the EAC is expected to present a good investment platform for both domestic and foreign investors due to their economies of scale. Benefits should also accrue to Uganda and Tanzania, who have, of late, reaped immensely from food commodity supply fluctuations in Kenya.

Introduction

The East African Community is the regional intergovernmental organisation of the Republics of Kenya, Uganda and Tanzania, with its Headquarters located in Arusha, Tanzania. The East African Heads of State signed the Treaty for the Establishment of the East African Community in Arusha on 30th November 1999.

The three East African countries cover an area of 1.8

million square kilometres and have a population of 82 million who share a common history, language, culture and infrastructure. These advantages provide the Partner States with a unique framework for regional co-operation and integration.

From Co-operation to Community

Prior to re-launching the East African Community in 1999, Kenya, Tanzania and Uganda had enjoyed a long history of co-operation under successive regional integration arrangements. These included the Customs Union between Kenya and Uganda in 1917, which the then Tanganyika later joined in 1927; the East African High Commission (1948-1961); the East African Common Services Organisation (1961-1967); the East African Community (1967-1977), and the East African Co-operation (1993-1999).

Institutions of the EAC

The main organs of the EAC are the Summit of Heads of State and or Government; Council of Ministers; Co-ordination Committee; Sectoral Committees; East African Court of Justice, East African Legislative Assembly; and the Secretariat.

The Region's External Trade

The region's principal exports are mainly agricultural products. These include horticulture, tea, coffee, cotton, tobacco, pyrethrum, fish, and hides and skins. Other exports include handicrafts and minerals such as gold, diamonds, gemstones, soda ash and limestone. Tourism is also one of the major sources of foreign exchange for the three countries.

The region's major imports are machinery and other capital equipment, industrial supplies and raw materials, motor vehicles and motor vehicle parts, fertiliser, crude and refined petroleum products.

The major trading partners of the region are the European Union, Japan, China, India, United Arab Emirates (UAE) and Saudi Arabia.

Development Strategy for EAC

The East African Community operates on the basis of a five-year Development Strategy. The Strategy document spells out the policy guidelines, priority programmes and implementation schedules.

The EAC strategy emphasises economic co-operation and development with a strong focus on the social dimension. The role of the private sector and civil society is considered as central and crucial to the regional integration and development in a veritable partnership with the public sector.

Areas of Co-operation

The regional co-operation and integration envisaged in the EAC is broad based, covering trade, investments and industrial development; monetary and fiscal affairs; infrastructure and services; human resources, science and technology; agriculture and food security; environment and natural resources management; tourism and wildlife management; and health, social and cultural activities.

Other areas of co-operation include free movement of factors of production; and co-operation in political matters, including defence, security, foreign affairs, legal and judicial affairs.

Partnerships

The EAC collaborates with other African organisations in the spirit of the Abuja Treaty for the establishment of the African Economic Community. Among these organisations are the African Union, Common Market for East and Southern Africa, Inter-governmental Authority on Development and the Southern African Development Community.

Funding

The core budget of the EAC's Secretariat is funded by equal contributions from the Partner States. Regional projects and programmes are funded through the mobilisation of resources from both within and outside the region.

Source: EAC and other sources.

Appendix II:

East African Federation

Towards an East African Federation: Debate, Rationale and Declaration of June 1963

After forty years of rejecting the federation, East African countries began demanding for it for several reasons.

First articulated by J.G. Kiano (later Minister for Commerce in Kenya) in September 1959; the reasons were three fold.

First, the European settler influence, which was strong in Kenya, would have extended throughout Uganda and Tanganyika thus complicating the struggle for independence in those territories.

Secondly, that the decision on when and if a federation was to take place was solely the business and responsibility of the African people and not of the white or the colonial office.

The third and perhaps the most important reason for a federation as stated in the June 1963 Declaration, was not only for the purposes of unity but a means of remedying the trade and industrial imbalances through economic planning under one federal government in East Africa. The Declaration stated:

"Thus the value of working together has been adequately demonstrated in the East African Common Services Organization and in the Common Market. But the scope of further joint action remains wide.

Economic planning, the maximum utilization of manpower and our other resources, the establishment of a central bank and common defence programme, and foreign and diplomatic representation, are areas in which we need to work together. Such an approach would provide greater co-ordination and savings in scare capital, facilities fro training and manpower. What is more, we would have a total of more than 25 million people-a formidable force and a vast market to influence economic development at home, attract a greater investment and enhance our prestige and influence abroad."

Accordingly, the Declaration set end of 1963 as a time when the federation would have been achieved, A timetable was published and a Working Party established to prepare a framework of a draft constitution of the East African Federation. The Working Party was to report back to a full conference of East African Governments that would sit in August 1963.

The Declaration gave rise to a spate of debates in the respective national assemblies of the three states.

In Uganda, as early as July 1963, reservations about the Motion supporting the federation were made. Indeed the Prime Minister of Uganda Milton Obote in October 1963 said:

"There are still points which Uganda believes must be settled before-and not after- the East African Federation is formed and which could explain why it (the federation) will not come into being this year."

Tanzania reacted to the prolonged talks over the Federation. During early 1964, Tanzania's Minister of External affairs Oscar Kambona stated:

"When we became independent in 1961 we acquiesced in a continuation of the existing arrangements for the common market-not because we believed that they were fair and equitable, but because we were prepared to treat them as an interim measure leading to eventual federation. If federation was to be postponed indefinitely, however, we could not continue to ignore the disadvantages to Tanganyika inherent in that common market."

On March 17, 1964, Tanganyika's Minister for Development Planning Nsilo Swai at a secret conference on the coordination of economic planning that sat at Entebbe, stated that his country was suffering economically for prolonged talks over the federation and proposed:

"To equalize the disadvantages of indefinite talking about federation by limiting trade with Kenya and Uganda through such devices as tariffs and import quotas."

Mwalimu Julius Nyerere, President of Tanzania, told the Central Legislative Assembly in August 1965:

"Let me stress again that Tanzania understands the economic problem of her neighbours and deeply regrets any temporary complication which her need creates. We have tried to avoid it. Although our problem was clear to us long before our independence, we took no action until 1964 because we hoped the matter could be dealt with in the framework for an East African Federation.

For a time we were willing and able to accept the status quo, and all its disadvantage to us, as a necessary price to pay for East African unity. But in the absence of any progress or any hope of any early federation, we had no alternative but to seek actively for an equalization of the advantages and disadvantages of the common market. Only when our efforts failed to bring practical agreement on an East African basis did we, reluctantly, take steps on our own."

The Nairobi Summit

Alarmed by the statements of the two Tanzanian Ministers Kambona and Swai, Kenya convened a meeting of Heads of Government in Nairobi (The Nairobi Summit) on April 10, 1964 to forge ways to end the existing trade imbalances and thereby facilitate progress towards political federation.

In a Communiqué issued at the end of the Summit, the Tanganyika delegation made an assurance that they had no intention of withdrawing from the East African Common Market. The Conference also agreed to set up an Emergency Committee to examine certain problems relating to trade relations within the 3 countries. The sentiments of the delegates especially the Kenyans were not disclosed at the Communiqué but were to be revealed in the Minutes of the Conference.

Jomo Kenyatta, then Prime Minister of Kenya and Chair of the Summit in his opening remarks stated:

"This meeting has been called to discuss the Tanganyika Governments's decision to leave the East African Common Market and Currency. Here in Kenya we are alarmed at the prospect of implementing this decision. On balance, we have accepted that Kenya gains most from the market.

We do not , however, admit that our gains are made at the expense of the other partners. Our examination shows that Kenya is rapidly losing its hare of these gains, oddly enough to Tanganyika. Besides, there are other advantages arising form East African Common Services and Raisman arrangements.

If it proves impossible to establish a Federation, we consider that the Common Market should be preserved for yet another year. We have just become independent, we have problems of unemployment....

I should like to command to you these thoughts. I hope prosperity will say that this meeting saved the Common Market; that the Common Market begot the Federation."

Dr. Julius Nyerere had this to say:

"Mr. Chairman, you stated in your opening remarks, that Tanganyika had decided to leave the Common Market. I wish to correct that statement. Tanganyika has made proposals to modify certain structural relationships and the problems posed by this are easy and simple: they do not involve withdrawal.

We have, however, inherited advantages and disadvantages in the Common Market. No one can be blamed or congratulated for these disadvantages and advantages inherent in the Common Market.

All the people who have studied the Common Market say it is very useful thing for East Africa. East Africa has gained industries, investments and an infrastructure as a result of the Common Market. Indeed, East Africa would not have been as attractive to investors overseas without it. If you break the Common Market, there is no doubt that East Africans would suffer.

There is however a paradox here. What is good for the whole should be good for the part. This is not true in economics. It is possible for the Common Market to serve East Africa as a whole without serving the component parts. There must be deliberate actions to redress the imbalances which may arise..........

The aim behind the establishment of the Common Market was that it should serve Kenya. Let me make it clear, however, that I am not blaming Kenya: it is the rulers of East Africa at the time who planned deliberately that Kenya should be the center of economic activity. They, at first wanted a federation; they could not get it, so they established the Common Market to serve their interests.

Now, there are certain rules which determine accumulation of investment and one of them is indicated in a passage in the Bible which says, (He who has more will be given and he who has not even that which he has will be taken away form him).

In so saying, Jesus was referring to facts of life. Kenya has developed more than Uganda and Tanganyika: the result is that we have only a legal common market, while in fact , it is Tanganyika which is the Common Market for all. Uganda and Kenya sell to Tanganyika more than Tanganyika sells to either of them and, therefore, Tanganyika is the Common Market of Kenya and Uganda. As such, it will be some time before we can have a true Common Market of the three East African countries.....

One-way of meeting Tanganyika's problem is to have some form of tariff protection. Another possible way might be to agree to limit the amount of goods which one country buys from another. Up to now, Tanganyika had not pressed this solution because it would be painful to Kenya who would have no market for her goods. Another method is that we could aim at reducing the trade imbalance gradually with a view to eliminating it in a given period...."

Dr. Apollo Milton Obote (Prime Minister of Uganda)

noted:

"At the end of the (Entebbe) meeting, the Tanganyika Delegation submitted a paper which was read to the meeting. We in Uganda took the paper as meaning that Tanganyika was going to walkout of the Common Market, and I think from the information available to me and now confirmed by what we have said in the meeting we had this morning, that Kenya felt that paper indicated that Tanganyika was desirous of leaving the Common Market....

I think we cannot now take the point of view of the Tanganyika Delegation at the Uganda meeting. I think we .can now take the point of view as expressed by the President this morning......."

However, the above economic and political bickering and tensions that characterized the East African co-operation was linked to the Chinese arms controversy of May 1965. On May 15, a convoy of trucks traveling from Tanzania to Uganda was seized at Kisii in Kenya near the common Tanzania, Uganda and Kenya border.

The convoy upon examination was found to be carrying 75 tons of Chinese arms and the 47 men accompanying the trucks, turned out to be Uganda army personnel and some civilian drivers. On May 21, Uganda and Tanzania threatened a complete break up of the East African Common Market unless Kenya released both the arms and personnel and facilitated their transit. The episode was amicably closed.

The Kampala Agreement 1964

The recommendations made by the Emergency Committee set up after the Nairobi Summit of April 1964, were approved and ratified by the Presidents of the 3 East

African countries, in Kampala in May 1964. This gave birth to an agreement, which was later modified in Mbale in Uganda in January 1965, and became known as the Kampala Agreement. The Emergency Committee had been set up to address the inter-territorial trade imbalances and comprised of the Ministers of Finance and of Commerce and Industry of the three countries. The Committee presented its report to the three heads of state as mandated, on May 23, 1964, in Nairobi.

The Agreement proposed 6 ways of redressing trade imbalances between the 3 East African countries:

a) Increased production in a deficit country by firms which operated in two or more countries

b) Partial re-allocation of some existing major industries in Kenya to Uganda and Tanzania through establishment of " branch " factories

c) The allocation of selected major new industries to the three countries

d) The application of a quota system to exports from a more industrially advanced Partner state

e) Increased sales from one country in deficit to a country in surplus

f) Early agreement within the East African Common Market on a system of inducements and allocation of industry in order to secure the equitable distribution of industrial development as between the three countries.

With regard to measure a), immediate action was taken. The Ministers of Commerce asked 4 East African companies, namely, East African Tobacco Company Limited, Bata Shoe Company Limited, Eat African

Breweries Limited and British Standard Portland Cement(Bamburi), which were operating in all the three states, to increase production of their products in the two deficit states of Tanzania and Uganda. All the four agreed. It was anticipated that if production was to increase as planned, it would reduce Tanzania's and Uganda's overall levels of imbalance with Kenya by about 25% in favour of each state and Tanzania's imbalance with Uganda by about 1%.

With regard to measure b), immediate allocation of the following major industries was made for exclusive development in a partner state:

*Motor vehicle Assembly and Manufacture:

Land Rovers, exclusive to Tanzania

Lorry and trucks, not exclusive Tanzania

* Bicycle Manufacture, exclusive to Uganda

* Electric Light Bulbs, exclusive to Kenya

*Radio Assembly and Manufacture, exclusive Tanzania

*Nitrogenous Fertilizers, exclusive to Uganda

* Motor vehicle Tyres and tubes, exclusive Tanzania

As regards measure c), it was agreed that at, the earliest opportunity, a system of quota restrictions on inter-territorial imports from a surplus country could be imposed by a deficit country if the deficit country had existing productive capacity. Some rules were made to regulate the operation of this measure. No comment was made to measure (d).

On measure e), it was agreed that future allocation of new industries and differential incentives to industry would be referred to a Committee of Industrial experts.

Kenya's conditionalities under the Agreement

The acceptance of the Committee's recommendations by Kenya and by implication the Kampala Agreement was subject to the following conditions that:

a) The East African Common Market would continue

b) The Common Services would continue

c) In particular, there would continue to be a common currency

d) All parties recognized the value of association in a Common Market in fostering the economic development of the whole area

e) All parties agreed that the Common Market could only survive if the benefits of economic development were fairly shared among them.

Some of the suggested measures were applied immediately. For instance Tanzania applied for the quota system soon after signing although it in the hurry to implement, omitted to submit the matter to the Quota Committee. Vehicle assembling or other manufacturing activities required long periods of planning and preparatory activities, as a result of which no measure was actually effected.

The Kampala Agreement was the first serious step taken to address the causes of inequitable industrial development in the East African Common Market. The core thrust of the Kampala Agreement cut across the existing regime of free trade in the Common Market.

The Agreement was intended to institutionalize free trade in those goods agreed to by the Partner states to be produced on an East African basis and to restrict to quotas inter-state trade in goods produced severally by each state. The Agreement introduced the classification of "East African goods" and " national goods" which later led to the introduction of a Transfer tax in the EAC. In so doing the Agreement attempted to introduce an industrial strategy for East Africa for the first time.

Unfortunately, Kenya never ratified the Agreement and never gave the reasons for her refusal. In effect, the Agreement died before the ink was dry. The partner states especially Tanzania, saw the failure of the Kampala Agreement in infancy as the death nail of the proposed Federation of East Africa.

Source: Kituo Cha Katiba, Makerere University, Kampala, Uganda.

***

EAC 'given' Six Years to Become Federation

By Adam Ihucha, Tanzania *Guardian*, Arusha, Tanzania

136

The Fast Track Committee on the proposed East African Federation has come up with a 'road map' that puts January 2010 as the most appropriate time for the unity.

Handing over a seven-chapter report to the East African Heads of State at the Arusha International Conference Centre yesterday, the chairman of the committee, Amos Wako said: "The committee recommends year 2010 as ideal for the federation of EA to be launched.

It would be appropriate time for the federal president, cabinet, members of parliament and chief justice and judges of the federal supreme court to be sworn in."

Wako further said his committee proposed that the period between 2010-2012 be considered as the consolidation phase of the federation, adding that during this period, member states should exercise rotational presidency among its sitting heads of state.

The committee was also in favour of an enlarged federal parliament, to be elected under a similar system used to pick the current members of the East African Legislative Assembly (EALA).

Wako, who is also the Attorney General of Kenya, said between 2010 and 2012, the electoral commission and other institutions provided for under the federal constitution should be established, with federal constituencies being delineated.

According to the 'road map', all elections should be held between January and March 2013.

"This road map is indicative. It should be emphasized that with political will and resources the time frame provided can be compressed to enable East African Federation to be realized much earlier," Wako noted.

To this end, he said, it was recommended that the discussions on the protocol on free movement of persons, labour, services and right of establishment and residence should start as early as next January with a view of concluding the protocol by June 2006.

The protocol on common market should also start in January 2005, with a view to concluding the protocol by December 2007, Wako said.

On the monetary policy, Wako said the co-coordinating committee of the Central Banks of the partner states should immediately start working on a detailed strategic plan to ensure the introduction of one currency for EA by December 2009.

The plan, according to the committee, should be approved by the heads of state at their summit meeting in November or December 2005.

The visionary purpose for the establishment of EA Federation is accelerated economic development in the shortest possible time.

"It is therefore against this background we recommend that a task force on the East African Economic Development Strategy be appointed," Wako noted.

In order to ensure that the federal constitution was in place, a constitutional commission should be appointed by July 2005 and by December 2007, it should come up with a draft preliminary constitution.

"The challenge now is for the three presidents of the partner states to provide the necessary, visionary and innovative leadership so that east Africans successfully match towards that destination," concluded Wako.

Shortly after receiving the report, the chairman of the summit, President Benjamin Mkapa, showered praise on the Fast Track committee members and assured them that their recommendations would be dealt with accordingly.

"Let us now deliberate it. At the March Summit, we should be able to tell East African people, when and how we would hand over our respective national sovereignty to the federation," Mkapa said.

On his part, Kenyan President Mwai Kibaki expressed his country's willingness and committment to ensure that the East African Federation dream was realized.

Supporting the proposed federation, Ugandan President Yoweri Museveni wondered why Africans worshipped the 'strength of others' but did not strive to attain their own power.

Burundian President Domitien Ndayizeye and Prime Minister of Rwanda, Bernard Mukuza were part of high-ranking government officials who attended the summit.

* SOURCE: *The Guardian*, Dar es Salaam, Tanzania, November 17, 2004.

***

East Africa to Become a Single State in 2010

The Nation, Nairobi, Kenya
27 November 2004

Zephania Ubwani
Arusha, Tanzania

Kenya is to join Uganda and Tanzania in a federal superstate - and the date for the union has been set as January 2010.

The Big Three East African countries will keep their own identities with national parliaments, presidents and flags. But they will share a federal Parliament and Cabinet, a chief justice and supreme court, and a superstate President, who will be chosen from the three countries by rotation.

Seats in the federal Parliament will be shared out on the basis of representation in the home countries and will therefore echo the power of each party in the individual states.

The date of 2010 was agreed yesterday by the three

East African presidents, who endorsed a timetable put forward by experts charged with fast-tracking regional reforms. Their proposals were endorsed by President Kibaki,Tanzania's President Benjamin Mkapa and Uganda's President Yoweri Museveni in the northern Tanzanian town of Arusha.

Welcoming the announcement, President Kibaki said: "It is my desire that East African integration be achieved in my lifetime. Our people are ready to embrace the federation because of its benefits and would welcome this move even before the 2010 calendar set out by the fast-tracking committee."

The President said the timetable was "a great honour to the founding fathers of East Africa who had a vision for the prosperity of the region".He went on: "Mwalimu Nyerere and Jomo Kenyatta had a vision to unite all East Africans and today we have the opportunity to embrace the ideals of East Africa".

The fast-tracking team, led by Attorney General Amos Wako, worked out how to speed up the start of the East African federation for the Heads of State's sixth summit.

A Press statement issued after the summit - also attended by Burundi President Dometien Ndayizeye and Rwanda prime minister Bernard Makuza - said the team had presented "a realistic plan of implementation".

Giving the timetable during his speech at the Simba Plenary Hall of the Arusha International Conference Centre, Mr Wako said the three presidents will hold an extraordinary summit in March next year to discuss the report and decide the way forward.

Immediately after that a campaign will be launched to sell the idea of political federation to the people of East Africa - emphasising its benefits.

Continuing with the countdown to federation, Mr Wakosaid that by January 2005:

- Holders of East African passports should be exempted

from immigration requirements within East Africa;

- The three countries should publish identification documents acceptable to them, which will be recognised at common borders to allow free movement of their citizens;

- Administrative structures should be in place to let citizens living along common borders to move freely across them;

- Clearing channels should be set up at borders and entry points for citizens of the three countries; and

- Fishing in Lake Victoria should take place without undue restrictions according to national boundaries but should take into account the environment and sustainability of the lake.

By July 2005, entry permits and work permits for citizens of three states should be standardised.

By August 2005, East Africa should be a single air space which should reduce air fares and travel time within East Africa.

A constitutional commission should be appointed in July 2005 to make a draft of a new federal constitution, which should be ready by December 2007.

Meanwhile, by December 2006, there should be East African identity cards for all citizens of the three countries.

Then during 2008, Mr Wako said, a constitutional forum of representatives from Parliaments of the partner states and members of the East African Legislative Assembly should debate and approve the constitution.

Then the Federation of East Africa will be launched in January 2010, with a federal president and Cabinet, members of the federal Parliament and the chief justice and judges of the Federal Supreme Court sworn into office.

From 2010 to 2012 will be a period of consolidation, with an electoral commission and other bodies provided for under the federal constitution be put in place.
Federal constituencies would also be marked out.

Finally, between January and March 2013, the first

elections for a new federal president and federal Parliament should take place.

Mr Wako said that to speed up the start of federation, the team made several other recommendations, including the restructuring the EAC Secretariat which is currently short of both money and people.

About the Author

John Ndembwike studied electrical engineering in college but also has great interest in writing.

He was born and brought up in Tanzania where he has also worked for many years in his field of electrical engineering. He also lived and worked in Botswana and South Africa for a number of years in the same field.

Besides engineering and writing, his fields of interest include electronics and computer science.

His travels to other African countries including Zambia and Zimbabwe and the years he spent in Botswana and South Africa played a major role in fueling his interest in writing about his country.

He feels that there is a need for more books about Tanzania in order to help people in other parts of the world learn more about this country, the largest in terms of area and population among the countries of East Africa which include Kenya and Uganda in the East African Community.

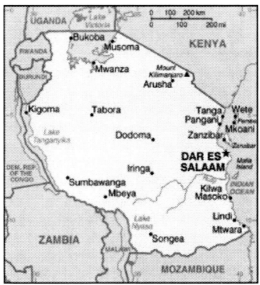
United Republic of Tanzania

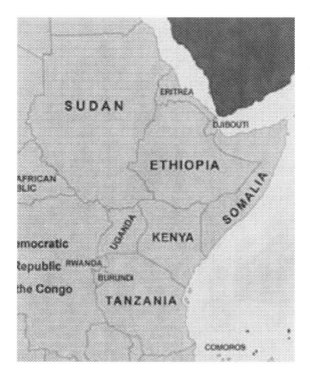

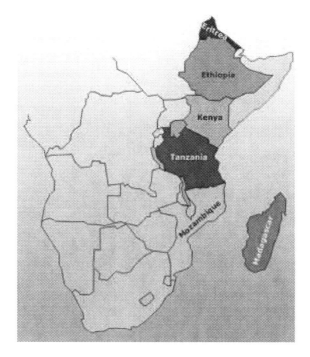

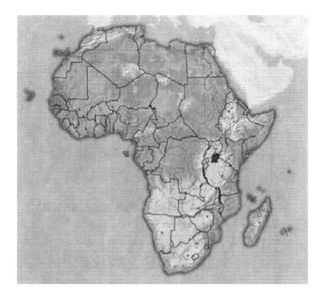

Alamance Community College
Library
P.O. Box 8000
Graham,NC 27253

Printed in the United States
207791BV00004B/13-15/A